Butterfly Boy

OTHER BOOKS BY RIGOBERTO GONZÁLEZ:

So Often the Pitcher Goes to Water until It Breaks (1999)

Soledad Sigh-Sighs (2003)

Crossing Vines (2003)

Antonio's Card (2005)

Other Fugitives and Other Strangers (2006)

Men without Bliss (2008)

The Mariposa Club (2009)

Camino del Sol: Fifteen Years on Latina and Latino Writing (editor, 2010)

Black Blossoms (2011)

Butterfly Boy

Memories of
a Chicano Mariposa

Rigoberto González

The University of Wisconsin Press

The University of Wisconsin Press
1930 Monroe Street, 3rd Floor
Madison, Wisconsin 53711-2059
uwpress.wisc.edu

3 Henrietta Street
London WC2E 8LU, England
eurospanbookstore.com

Printed in the United States of America

Library of Congress Cataloging-in-Publication Data
González, Rigoberto.
Butterfly boy: memories of a Chicano mariposa / Rigoberto González.
p.   cm. — (Writing in Latinidad)
ISBN 0-299-21900-3 (cloth: alk. paper)
1. González, Rigoberto.   2. Authors, American — 20th century — Biography.
3. Hispanic American gays — Biography.   I. Title.   II. Series.
PS3557.O4695Z46   2006
813'.54 — dc22   2006006990

ISBN 978-0-299-21904-8 (pbk.: alk. paper)
ISBN 978-0-299-21903-1 (e-book)

PARA MI FAMILIA

porque a veces los "quero"
y a veces "nigüas"

Of curse I love my father.

typo in an email to a friend

Children begin by loving their parents; after a time they judge them; rarely, if ever, do they forgive them.

Oscar Wilde

Contents

CONTENTS

Part 4: Zacapu Days and Nights of the Dead

Part 5: Unpinned

Acknowledgments

Excerpts from this book have been published in *Analecta* (as "Guitar Lessons," winner of the Nonfiction Essay National Competition); *Blue Mesa Review* (as "Ms. Burnett"); *Crab Orchard Review* (as "Piña" and "Our Secret Other Worlds," winner of the John Guyon Prize for Literary Nonfiction, also cited in *Best American Essays 2000*), edited by Jon Tribble; *Creative Nonfiction* (as "Liberace's Sink"), edited by Ilan Stavans; *The Literary Review* (as "A Home That Won't Refuse Me"), edited by Walter Cummins; in the anthology *Mama's Boy: Gay Men Write About Their Mothers,* New York: Painted Leaf Press, 2000 (as "Missing Mother"), edited by Dean Kostos and Eugene Grygo; in the anthology *Walking Higher: Gay Men Write About the Deaths of Their Mothers,* Xlibris: Print on Demand, 2004 (as "Canción Para Mi Madre/ Mother's Song"), edited by Alexander Renault; and in the anthology *Wonderlands: Good Gay Travel Writing,* Madison: University of Wisconsin Press, 2004 (as "Destino"), edited by Raphael Kadushin.

Many, many thanks to the folks at the Hawthornden Castle International Retreat for Writers in Scotland—what a timely gift! Grazie, Lella Telloli Heins, for our lengthy and inspiring chats on the island of Itaparica and in o mar brasileiro—your words brought mine to life. Muito obrigado, Fundaçao Sacatar, for that timely—albeit strained—two-month residency in Bahia. My gratitude also goes to the John Simon Guggenheim Memorial Foundation for the valuable travel money, and to Lauro Flores and Christine Yuodelis-Flores for giving me a home in Seattle (repeatedly!) when I didn't have one. I owe a great debt to Raphael Kadushin, Bino Realuyo, Sergio Troncoso, Ilan Stavans, Richard Rodriguez, and to my soul sisters Maythee and Lizzy Rojas for encouraging this journey with their kindness. Abrazos, Eric-Christopher García, Ondine Chavoya, and Michael S. Warren—many thanks for cariño y amistad. In spirit, Ying-She Chen. In memory, Roxana Rivera. I must also acknowledge David Bergman and Ricco Villanueva Siasoco, shrewd readers, for their insights. Finally I wish to express my appreciation to those people who have kept in touch via phone or email—I am indeed blessed by your friendships.

Smarting Points,
Starting Points

Summer's Passage, Southern California, 1990

Butterflies, my lover calls it, the art he places on my back. He locks his lips on each shoulder blade and sucks the skin, leaving deep red, almost purple hickeys that he says resemble wings. One butterfly on the left side and one on the right, and then he works his way down to the middle of the spine: a trail of love bites. He perfects his craft over months, after that first accidental mark on a vodka and crystal meth night.

"I just gave you another butterfly," he says. And I know then we are meant for each other because his gift matches my fantasy tattoo: I want a path of monarchs spiraling out of the base of my back and spreading open like a tornado, the insects growing in size as they flutter up toward my shoulders. Monarchs, I tell him, remind me of home and of my family.

"But I thought you hated home and your family," he says.

"But I love them too," I say.

My lover gives me butterflies on those sheet-twisting nights of sex and sweat. I learn to bear, and even welcome, the pain of his mouth. Each time his lips take hold of my skin I squirm beneath him, resisting the urge to push away as my flesh tightens and tingles. My eyes close and I clench my teeth. I tell myself this is the man who loves me, who has taught me the intimacy of his body and his bed without condition, who has put an end to my loneliness. I will never leave him.

The declaration sounds extreme, but that's how I've always heard it done in those Mexican ballads: smoky-voiced women belt out hyperbolic assertions with such conviction that even if their words compose impossible tasks, they seem binding and incontestable. At least in that moment.

I never ask my lover for butterflies and neither does he seek permission. He simply draws new ones as soon as the old ones fade out.

"Just make sure they don't reach above my neck," I remind him. "I don't want anyone else to see them."

He complies. Always the butterflies are the secret between us, like a private language, and it gives me pleasure to press myself against the back of a desk chair to sense the fresh prints of my lover's heat while I'm taking notes in a college classroom.

Since my lover works long hours, I have learned to wait. I study or read on those afternoons after classes, knowing that my lover is just as anxious to see me. Homework and research and academic papers are but distractions, a way of keeping time until the phone rings. And then he calls, sometimes at eight, sometimes at nine, and I drop everything for him. How perfect that the watch keeping time on my right wrist is a gift from him. The black leather band and convex glass over the pearl-colored face make me feel elegant. The heavy platinum watch my father gave me two years ago was tacky, and I was more than pleased when I lost it in a public restroom just two months after wearing what felt like a manacle. My lover's watch is prettier, more delicate, but it has been tightening like a handcuff as well.

Everything changes. I don't remember the first time at all. I don't remember when those marks on my body became fiery bruises, when his fist against my skin became part of our lovemaking. Sometimes he forgets why he has given me those wounds, and he kisses them with apology. Sometimes he surprises himself with the discovery of them.

"What's this?" he asks, tracing a new find after taking off my shirt.

I don't answer.

He wraps his arms around me, as if protecting me from himself. "It looks like a butterfly," he says. And I forgive him immediately. But not this time.

I slip my crooked glasses over my face. Seeing clearly doesn't do much to assuage the stinging in my eyes. My eyeballs ache from the furious crying the night before, after I told my lover I was leaving him for good. In our one-and-a-half-year history this will be breakup number three. My throat is hoarse from the screaming, my ears continue to buzz from listening to his. Through the sticky eyelashes, my lover's bedroom looks unfamiliar somehow, as if I've never been here before. My mind has begun to erase all memory of my stays. Even my lover's smell intoxicates; I detect him through the odor of liquor and pot. He's wearing his old cologne again, in defiance of my allergy to alcohol-based scents. The rash on my arms and torso are his fault.

As I look around the room to make sure I'm taking everything that belongs to me, my lover stirs awake. Like me he sleeps on his stomach; when he flexes, two dimples form just below his shoulders.

"So when are you coming back?" he asks, his voice muffled.

"I'm not," I reply in a hostile tone, perhaps to remind him of where we left off the night before.

"Don't be a bitch," he says, "I mean when are you coming back from México?"

I relax, but I'm disappointed that he's so easily accepted my leaving this morning. The entire time I'm dressing he looks at me through the one eye exposed; the rest of his face remains pressed against the pillow. In the corner, another week's worth of the unread *Press Enterprise* lays stacked and abandoned. I catch the familiar mugs of President Bush and Vice President Quayle on the front page.

"I don't know," I say. "I may decide to stay away the entire summer."

I'm not surprised we haven't had this conversation before. When I brought it up last night it was part of my threat, not my lament. It's as if we were both looking forward to an undetermined length of

5

separation, a respite from the stress of stubbornly holding on when it's clear the relationship is over.

I expect him, however, to protest a little, or at the very least to seize this final opportunity before my exit to suggest that we should talk when I return or that I should stay in touch, but again his silence disappoints me. This break-up isn't following the pattern of all the other ones we've had. There's no pleading after the fight and the fuck.

I tie my shoes slowly. Still no response from my lover. For a moment I think he has fallen asleep, so I intend to make some noise to wake him up. But when I look, he's still face down, staring at me through his eye. He's being unfair because I can't read his expression that way. I can't tell if he's angst-ridden under there or staring at me coldly.

"I'll walk back to my apartment," I say.

"I wasn't offering a ride," he says. I feel the sting all over. And then comes his dare, "Is something holding you back?"

I shake my head. We've done all the insulting and humiliating the night before. I accused him of cheating on me and he called me jealous and possessive. Both are true. I threw his alarm clock against the wall and he punched me on the chest, my body falling into pieces like the plastic clock after it struck the hard surface, its bright red numbers going black. And somewhere between the slap on the face and the spitting of words we wedged in our soft tongues and the cooing. I cling to the memory of his hairy body grating against my smooth skin, but the image suddenly gets swallowed up by the one in which he grabs my hair to make sure I look at him when he swears at me in Spanish. In Spanish our voices are much more violent because the hatred comes from the gut, not from the schools of our adopted second language.

I find more clues to the night before: a cleared mantel with a pile of photographed faces to one side of the fireplace; my lover's belt with its buckle looking wide-mouthed in exhaustion; the hastily torn condom packet and the dented tube of K-Y with its cap two inches away like a broken tooth; one of my textbooks with its covers spread apart against the wall. Its ruffled pages make it look like pigeon roadkill. I can't remember if that last object was his act of rage or mine.

When I look into the mirror to fix my hair, I notice a crust of dry blood inside the ring of my nostril. I scratch the flakes off with my thumb. This wound is unintentional: my nose struck my lover's shoulder when we rolled around in bed during the scuffle and embrace of sex.

I don't have to hold back tears because I don't have any to offer anyway when I finally say good-bye to my lover who now looks inoffensive and tempting in his dark nakedness. His strong arms appear defeated and this fills me with sadness because they're the feature of his that I admire the most. They're the parts of his body I reach for when I wake up in the middle of the night and I want to remind myself that my lover, all muscle and strength, is still in bed beside me.

Out of habit I'm about to say, "I'll call you later," but I hold in the phrase just in time and it drops like a weight inside me. Instead I pick up the damaged textbook and slip it into my backpack along with my socks and the extra underwear I keep in one of the cherry wood drawers. I don't want to search through the stack of photographs for the one of me standing on the dock of Redondo Beach, the dock that burned down months after our visit. So I let it remain in the rubble as a dramatic symbol of what is now no longer. I debate about the watch. I take it with me.

As I walk out of the bedroom I make sure to leave the door ajar so that I may hear my lover no matter how softly he may speak. But all I pick up by the time I reach the front door is the slight snoring that I have grown accustomed to, that has given me peace of mind on those uncertain nights when I wondered if my father even thought of me anymore.

I close the door behind me. I test the knob. Yes, I've definitely locked myself out.

Walking from his place to mine is a surprisingly short distance. We both live off Blaine Street, a strip of housing complexes with cheap student housing. He lives there because he's a professional and can afford his own place; the rest of us contend with roommates. It has taken me a while to admit that this proximity to younger men is also a matter of interest to him.

The temperature is already warm at eight in the morning and the day is clear and sunny, as if anything can come to light. But none of these college kids heading on foot toward the university can even guess the secrets I keep. This makes me want to scream at them. And then a thought strikes me. This morning, with a backpack over my own shoulder, I blend in. I'm one of them. So I continue my trek home as if there is nothing out of place in my head.

I expect the phone to ring the entire time I'm packing in my apartment. But there's no ring. I call a cab, leave a note for my room-mate along with next month's rent, and arrive at the Riverside Grey-hound station on Market Street just ten minutes before the next bus to Indio, 90 miles south into the Coachella Valley. I picture my lover sinking into the bed as if he were deflating like a prop in a movie set.

How quickly I slip from one world to another, I think on the bus as it circles around the station en route to Highway 10. In Riverside I'm a college sophomore majoring in the humanities and no one knows I'm involved with an older man who makes love to me as fiercely as he angers me. In Indio I'm the son and grandson of farmworkers who have never once hugged me, but whom I miss terribly, espe-cially when I need to run away from the man who tells me that he loves me, he loves me, he loves me.

On a direct route, the trip between Riverside and Indio takes about an hour. On the Greyhound, which makes stops at all the little towns in between, the journey will stretch out to four hours. I'm drowsy enough to nap, but my shoulder bothers me when I press my weight against it. Behind me, two old men chat in Spanish about the rising tensions in the Middle East, and about what a better pres-ident Ronald Reagan was than his successor. Their drone knocks me out temporarily, and I'm grateful that I'm not possessed by the urge to kill myself. Again I'm resorting to the desperation in those Mexican heartbreak songs. The other times I broke up with my lover that seemed like the only next step though I never took it. This time I have a direction. South.

Welcome to Indio, California, Pop. 36,793

There's nothing like a bus ride out of town after a lovers' quarrel to make a person sentimental about getting home to family. This trip to Indio is only the first step toward a longer journey into México, into the state of Michoacán, into the town of Zacapu, where my father was born, where my mother was raised, and where I grew up. The visit will be more significant because I'll be turning twenty while I'm there. As I take in the low desert scenery of sparse brush and cracked topsoil, I can't help but look forward to the lush greenery and fertile mountains of the homeland. When the bus passes Windy Point, just south of Palm Springs, the energy windmills shoot up from the barren panorama. The windmills are huge white shafts with three blades that spin like propellers but at slow speed. They remind me of cartoon stick figures running in place. By the time the field of giants disappears in the horizon behind me, I've made a mental list of my goals for the summer:

I will not fight with my father.
I will not long for my lover.
I will forgive my father.
I will forget my lover.

Never have simple sentences seemed so complicated. As my eyes water I can't make up my mind about what's making me cry: the possibility that I will indeed never go back to my lover, or the possibility that my father and I will finally reconcile. I'm grateful I decided weeks ago to entertain my father's offer. His second wife and their children have gone to Michoacán ahead of him, and since I had been planning a visit to my maternal grandparents, wouldn't it make sense for my father and me to be traveling companions?

"Are you sure you know what you're getting into?" my brother, Alex, warned me on the phone when I told him about my plans.

"I think I'm ready," I replied. "And don't forget," I quickly added, "I need to pick up that photograph I let you guys borrow."

"Let's talk about that when you get here," Alex said.

"What? What happened?" I asked, panic in my voice.

"Just wait," he said.

Minutes from the center of town I begin to get nervous. How frightening to expect that things will be different when the flat town of Indio itself looks unchanged year after year. There's a fancy new gas station near the first major off-ramp, but the vehicles are the same beat-up trucks and cars with dented doors that the farmworkers drive to and from the agricultural fields. The long lines at the pumps can only mean that the crews have stopped working for the day. Any of these people scrambling about for water to quench their thirst could be someone I'm related to. Any of these bodies wincing at the trappings of their hot clothing could have been me. I feel lucky that this was not my fate.

I shut my eyes to look past this scene, this town, and even this country, reaching back to the place where I keep my early memories. Sentimentalizing is my only recourse, especially since I know that within the hour I will have to face my father. What gives me courage is remembering the man he used to be. What disheartens me is knowing the man he has become. I imagine my mother in moments like these. She was always staring out the windows of our many residences over the years, waiting for my father to get home. Had my father known she was not going to live a long life, he might have gotten home sooner instead of staying out drinking. I particularly remember her hair, shoulder-length and wavy, because on so many evenings of her sadness and patience, I stood behind her, unnoticed.

Later, as my cab pulls into the Fred Young Farm Labor Camp off Van Buren Avenue, my mind switches completely to Spanish and the stress begins to build inside me. This is my grandparents' apartment, but my father stays here through the grape harvest. He spends the rest of the year with his new family in Mexicali, just south of the California border. My younger brother, Alex, who dropped out of high school, is now living that same cycle: México, United States, México, United States, work and rest, work and rest. When I enter the door to the cinderblock building, my grandfather greets me. He has just dyed his hair pitch black. I expect to find the stained toothbrush he uses on his mustache in the bathroom sink.

"You're here?" he asks. "You need a haircut, you?" No one but my grandfather ever cuts my hair, which is why my visits to Indio usually coincide with my need for a trim.

"Later," I say. "No one's back from work?"

"I'm surprised," my grandfather says, already serving me a plate of chicken in rice noodles without asking if I'm hungry. And although I'm not hungry I'll still eat. It's all part of the ceremony of my homecoming. The long tattoo of a colorful peacock that he carries on the inside of his forearm glares out at me from the kitchen.

"It's nearing the end of the season, so they're usually finished early these days," he adds.

As soon as I sit down at the table, my father's 1974 blue Mustang pulls into the driveway. My brother is behind the wheel. My grandmother sits in the front passenger seat. She's the only one still wearing the dusty bandanna over her hair. After all these years she continues to color coordinate to pick grapes; the purple bandanna matches her sweatshirt. My father is the first to step out of the car. When they enter they respond to my presence without surprise. In our family we have never been good at expressing affection when we're sober, and there's never any physical contact—not a handshake, not a hug—and I have never seen anyone offer a kiss, except for my mother, who's been dead for over eight years. So my father, my grandmother, and my brother walk awkwardly into the apartment, smelling of sulfur and radiating body heat, and simply nod toward me to acknowledge a welcome.

Only my grandmother speaks up. "You're here?" she says. "You need a haircut, you?"

When my father passes by, my body stiffens. I tell myself to relax. I shove a spoonful of food into my mouth. The swamp cooler has kept the room temperature down but beads of sweat still collect at my hairline. Through the curtains I see other vehicles pulling into parking spots and dusty bodies slowly exiting the cramped cars.

My grandmother sits down on the couch to drink a beer and my grandfather starts to tinker with the pots over the stove. I have slipped inside the daily routine of the farmworkers and it makes me feel I'm in the way. I don't belong here anymore. The familiar claustrophobia begins to take hold of me; I used to suffer from it for years before I finally got out. The crowded walls are no help. For as long as I can remember my grandmother has been nailing every piece of gaudy memorabilia into the concrete, from family photographs to meat market calendars to the cheap Mother's Day presents my brother and I have given her over the years.

"So you're going to Zacapu, you?" my grandmother asks before she lets out a small belch. When she says the name of our hometown her eyes light up.

"Yes. And I can stay there all summer if I want," I tell her. My tone is intentionally malicious, a way to remind her that I'm now free to travel wherever I want to go and she's not because my grandfather still keeps her like a prisoner. She knows this. She sinks back into a tired silence. It's much easier for her to turn the television on and stare empty-eyed into the screen than to deal with my usual antics, so she leans over to reach for the knob.

Ashamed, I clear my plate and walk across the living room to do the first thing I said I'd do once I arrived: reclaim that photograph.

The photograph is an old black-and-white one I inherited from my mother. The shot was taken back in 1969 when my parents were newlyweds. It shows my father, age twenty-three, in his slimmer, healthier youth, and my mother, age nineteen, in her youthful beauty, her face round and graceful. Their skin tones contrast nicely. My father's dark, my mother's light. I kept the photo tucked safely inside a book over the years, afraid it would be damaged by the sticky backings of our flimsy photo albums. Even when my father asked for it repeatedly, saying he wanted to have it blown up, I refused to let it go. But then he had the excuse that I was no longer living at home and that I might lose it, moving around the way I did. So I agreed with much trepidation to let him borrow it back in December.

While my father showers, my brother breaks the bad news: it's been ruined. Since it was a 5 x 7, the photograph could not fit inside any regular envelope, so we had settled on a red one made specifically for a Christmas card. The match was perfect and the color gave it a level of conspicuousness that ensured it wouldn't be lost so easily. But the logic backfired: somehow the envelope had made an inviting coaster and someone had placed a wet glass of water on top of it. The ink had run through and my parents' faces look bloodied and wounded.

"I don't understand," I tell Alex as he hands me the picture. "What the fuck was he going to do with it after he blew it up?" My brother and I are the only ones who communicate in English, which we only speak when we're alone. We're the same height and wear the same shoe size, but we resemble each other in no other way.

"I don't know," my brother says. "Put it up on his wall, I guess."

We both know my father's second wife would never let that happen.

When my father, shirtless and dripping water from the strands of his hair, comes into the room, he looks up and down at me before he concludes, "You lost weight, you." Each time I see him bare like this I'm surprised anew by the presence of tattoos on his body, the

14

greenish tint of the clover on his shoulder barely visible on his dark skin.

"*This* is how you fucking take care of things? Who the fuck did this?" I yell, waving the picture at him. From the corner of my eye I can tell my brother is amazed at how I waste no time. At five-foot-five, I'm much taller than my father, and this gives me a false sense of power and authority over him in moments like these.

"It was an accident," he says. "It was nobody's fault."

"Yes, it was *my* fault," I say. "For letting you have the picture!"

"I said it was nobody's fault," he insists. "Why don't you just leave things alone for once?"

"And what? Ignore that this picture is damaged? What do you want me to do from now on, pretend it always looked this way?"

"You're making a big deal out of this," he says.

"It's a huge deal to me!" I say, my voice shaky, my hand trembling. I'm upset that my father isn't. "I can't believe you let this happen! I can't believe—"

"Why don't you shut up?" he interrupts, his voice low and firm. "What happened to this photograph hurts me much more than it does you."

And with that retort I feel as if he's kicked me in the stomach because I know it's true, so I throw the photograph at him and it bounces off his beer belly. In the living room my grandparents are sitting close to each other like a pair of plump hens. When they see me storming out in anger they both say at once, "Already?"

"Already?" they ask, because this is also a part of the homecoming ceremony, though the fighting with my father has never happened so quickly. As soon as I walk out into the desert heat I feel like a fool. I have nowhere else to run and the sun is blazing. In fact, didn't I just flee somewhere else to get to here? I'm like a child in a tantrum, and for a fleeting second I think about how my lover put up with this kind of behavior all year. Is *this* why I get my ass kicked in Riverside? I shake that thought out of my head. I need to stop thinking like that. And then I keep thinking like that. My lover hits me, though my father has never dared to. My grandfather was the one who used to lay his hands on me, on all of us. Why don't I feel that level of rage for *him?* Why am I so cruel to everyone else?

My head continues to spin so I drop down on my knees in a dramatic display of grief. And how silly my theater is, I conclude, because behind me the apartment is all windows and clear curtains, and full of the faces of people who have never learned after all these years how to rush over to a person in distress in a noble attempt at rescue.

In the hot silence a radio forces out the sound waves of a song that reminds me of the times I picked grapes alongside my family. I was never good at it, my hands so small and clumsy. I have my mother's hands. I heard she was never good at picking either. One of my hands can disappear inside my lover's fist. I want to press my hands to my ears. How I hate that song with its jovial accordion and a singer whose falsetto tears down the distance between the work fields I never wanted to come back to and me.

I get up and dust my knees. Yet another déjà vu: I'm in the fields, beneath the grapevines. To reach the low bunches, I have to get down and sink into the hot soil. Even with the thick denim the heat comes through and my joints become as numb as my head. How I wished for the days to be old enough to go away and never have to suffer pain like this. As I walk into the living room again I know I haven't ventured very far because I'm back. And I keep going back.

Ghost Whisper to My Lover

Maybe this will explain, querido, why I keep returning to my father.

It's 1975 and my father is the bass player for Dinastía, a band that plays throughout the state of Michoacán, but which is mainly in demand locally in our hometown of Zacapu. They perform for weddings, baptisms, graduations, quinceañeras, and anniversary parties. On occasion my mother, who stays home to care for my younger brother, lets me tag along to the band's engagements, on the condition that I not wander off and that I stay within my father's line of sight. At five years old, I'm curious but cautious about straying far from the stage, where I know my father keeps a watchful eye.

After much fine-tuning and fuss over the lighting, electrical plugs, and wiring, the band starts their performance. The speakers blare out into the crowds now stirred into quick motion. Some people take a partner, others gyrate without one, but then the bodies converge on the dance space into a single moving mass, heads bobbing and elbows swinging as if tossing around in water. I make a feeble attempt at dancing cumbia, slightly bending my knees to the rhythm. But by the middle of the show, I grow weary; staring at so much vigorous activity absorbs my energy. I find a place to nap close to the stage, and then I roll my body beneath the wooden platform, where the vibrations lull me and assure me that my father is close by, hovering above me, in fact, like a moth, or the moon.

I fall asleep.

The dream: I'm completely naked. The band members have reached the pinnacle of their enthusiasm and so has the audience, responding wildly to the riffs of the music. I'm possessed by the excitement and jump into the middle of the stage, my baby penis exposed and my dimpled hand waving a two-finger V. The crowd cheers and greets me with a parade of peace symbols. I continue to negotiate the maze of wires and cords as I prance around barefoot, further motivated by the crowd's reaction to my presence. Suddenly, the song comes to an end, the speakers let go of the final note like the string to a kite, and the crowd shrinks into silence. A lonely feminine voice soars through the haze of lighting and demands: "Let him speak!" A burst of whistling and applause follows.

I become paralyzed. I feel my father come up from the back of the stage. He has pulled a microphone from its stand and taps it twice to confirm it's functioning. He kneels behind me and pushes the microphone to my face. With the guitar still strapped to his torso, he moves in closer, and the strings stinging my backbone edge me forward.

"Say something," my father whispers, simply a voice now, permeable and elusive as smoke.

The faces in the crowd grow like balloons. The widening eyes mock me. There I stand, naked, scared, with my father hiding behind me, leaving me vulnerable to these strangers. I succumb to the urge to urinate and release a stream—a weak arc of yellow that glitters with the stage lights.

I wake up to the sound of applause. The band has just finished playing another number. My crotch is damp and warm. I scurry out from under the stage to find my father and I'm surprised that he isn't looking for me. An anxious gaze distorts my face as I consider waving my arm to get my father's attention, but I know this won't work because he's too distracted at the moment. My father keeps his smile fixed on his audience—his mouth, all teeth, all satisfaction, all bliss. Is that my father? *I ask myself. And the answer fills me with a wonder I have never experienced before.*

Now Leaving Mexicali, Baja California, Norte

The Mexicali bus station is bustling with people, some dragging their luggage across the floor by a strap like a pet on a leash, others sitting as they fan themselves to cool off, their suitcases prone like coffins at their feet. The grainy voice over the speakers announces gate numbers, schedule changes, arrivals, and departures in a flat, disinterested tone that seems to ridicule the level of anxiety in the lobby. Armed policemen walk about with a sense of purpose though visibly bored, and the taxi drivers accost anyone with a packed bag.

"Taxi, amigos?" a man in a yellow guayabera asks us as we stand at the entrance of the station, trying to figure out where to go.

My father waves him away.

"Where are you headed?" the taxi driver insists. "I'll make you a good deal."

"Michoacán," my father says.

The driver quickly turns to a couple with a child in tow passing by. "Taxi, amigos?" he asks them.

"First class is in the other lobby," I point out. My shirt is sticky on my skin. For some reason I decided to wear white and I'm dismayed I've already collected grime on the brief car ride to the station. The blue Mustang will stay parked at my aunt's old house, though I doubt it will remain unused. I can already picture my cousins joyriding into the sleepiest hours of the night. When they dropped us off at the bus station I detected that mischievous glint in their eyes.

"I don't have enough money for first class, you," my father informs me. My body spasms, giving me a clear signal that this is the start to another bad ending.

"Well, I don't want to take a bus that's going to break down halfway to Michoacán," I say.

"But first class is a waste," he argues. "What are you paying for, a can of soda? Some stale peanuts?"

"No, I'm paying for a working toilet and air-conditioning."

"But I can't afford first class," he says.

"I can," I say.

"So you're going to pay for a first-class ticket when second class is half the price?"

"Absolutely," I insist.

"You could buy two tickets with that money."

"Look," I say, exasperated. "I can let you borrow some money for your ticket as well, just make sure you get good seats."

"Give me the money, then," he says.

I hand over the money because I don't want to hassle with the lines. I'm already hot and uncomfortable, and the constant flow of people has begun to make me edgy. *Engentarse,* my grandmother calls this claustrophobia that comes from getting swallowed up by a flood of people. I stand over our bags like a chicken roosting over a nest. My father returns fifteen minutes later.

"You bought second-class tickets!" I complain as soon as I look at the flimsy paper stubs.

"You said you were going to pay for my ticket. And I'm going second class, so I bought one for you as well. Aren't we traveling together? Here, I saved you some money. Can I borrow it until we get to Michoacán?"

Unbelievable, I think as I shake my head. My father has done it to me again. But I let it go. It'll be my give to his take this time. We've had plenty of practice this past week: I took the photograph and he

20

didn't protest; he asked for gas money for the ride from Indio to Mexicali and I opened my wallet; I told him I didn't want to talk during the one-and-a-half-hour car ride to the border and he kept his mouth shut.

We make our way to the gate, nonrefundable tickets in hand. The run-down bus waits at the end of the station, edged out like the runt of the litter by the newer buses. I suspect our bus will stop at every town with a station en route from Baja California to Michoacán to load and unload passengers. At that pace, the trip will take over three days, maybe four. Incensed, I make my father take the aisle seat. I want the advantage of the window, but to my dismay, it doesn't open. I scowl at my father.

"Now what?" he says.

"It smells in here," I say.

"I don't smell anything," my father says.

"No, of course not," I reply.

The cramped bus begins to incite my claustrophobia so I stare out through the green glass to watch the soda and pork rind sellers gravitating like bees toward the bus windows, their goods precariously balanced on tin platters. Despite the condition of the bus, I'm glad to be safely inside, away from the flurry. More people climb on board, filling up the bus with bodies, boxed packages, a crying baby and whining children, and the odors of armpits, evaporating perfumes, and oily foods. When the bus finally pulls out of its parking space, I breathe a sigh of relief. The journey back to Michoacán has officially started. For the last decade I've been going back and forth between México and the United States an average of every three years; the length of each stay varies depending on the temperament of my adult companions. My father likes the long stays, my grandfather loses steam quickly and heads back to the States on a whim. Regardless, I feel a sense of renewal each time I depart, as if whatever has happened up to then could be left behind like belongings too bulky to take along. I look forward to emerging from the bus at the last stop, stretching out my arms to a new beginning.

My disposition begins to soften as the bus slowly inches forward. I even turn to my father and exchange a complicit smile. He throws in a knowing nod for effect. An open window a few seats up begins to ventilate the acrid odor of sweat mixed with the polluted fumes. "Here we go," I declare with childish excitement. If this journey were a musical, this scene would be the perfect place to break into song. As if on cue, the bus driver turns the radio on. Los Tigres del Norte—or one of the group's many imitators—plays an upbeat norteño, heavy on the brass. The tune isn't exactly what I have in mind, but it will do. Suddenly I'm easy to please. I make myself comfortable against the itchy seat, relax my head against the rest, and sigh once more.

And then the bus pulls over to the side to let the first-class buses exit first.

"Santa mierda," I say. I'm positive I'm not the only one on board to curse.

When the bus driver turns off the noisy engine, the music grows obnoxiously loud. The old bus stands parallel to the back wall like an overworked boom box sentenced to the misery of its cheap speakers.

When I look over at my father he grins apologetically. I can say something now or save it for later. Since I get motion sickness when I read, I don't bother bringing a book on board with me. Speaking to my father will be the only way to kill time. He'll be the intimidating tome I get through by consuming it piecemeal. Except that I'll be forced to reckon with my father more frequently since he's sitting next to me on a bus. I cannot escape him. I decide to save my complaint for later.

When the bus finally squeezes out of the station, picking up speed as it makes its way through the blackened façades of Mexicali, the tension in my muscles begins to ease. It takes only minutes for the bus to reach the outskirts of the city; the arid desert looks reddish and damp through the green tint of the glass. And once I'm visibly relaxed, my father pipes up as if he's been waiting to seize the moment. He asks me abruptly, "Do you remember your mother?"

I hate it when my father comes at me like that. Invoking the memory of my mother is the fastest way to make me raise my defenses.

"Of course," I say, slightly indignant. I immediately turn my entire body toward the window, my reflection superimposed on the passing desert and a row of wooden shacks with clothes on the lines that look like party decorations the day after the party.

"You must never forget her," he says.

I see my chance. "You mean like you did," I say.

"I haven't forgotten your mother," he says in alarm. "Why do you say that?"

I think the answer is obvious so I don't bother with it.

I focus on a child bent over a basin with water. He stares out at the passing bus as if he has to pose for the passengers because in the next instant he's gone, quickly forgotten. On the glass I see my father pinch the small scar on the right side of his chin. He had a mole removed a few years back because he kept cutting it open when he shaved. Now he fondles the flesh when lost in thought—a habit he didn't have when the mole was still there.

"Does your grandfather still work in the mercado in Zacapu, you?" he asks.

"Don't change the subject," I say. "And quit asking me these dumb questions. You know he still works there."

"Look, son," he says to me in the low tone he adopts when he grows serious. "We don't need to start the trip like this. We have three days to go and plenty of time to throw punches, so can't we just have a friendly conversation for now?"

Bajar la cresta, my grandmother calls the act of calming down your anger. I picture the agitated rooster lowering its neck, the corolla of neck feathers folding down, his comb becoming flaccid.

I nod my head in agreement. My fingernails are already dirty, the edges looking like inked-in frowns. My father tries to chat again but I'm not in the mood, so I simply rest my head against the window and close my eyes. I want to remove my glasses, but without them I can't see the view through the window each time I open my eyes, so I leave them on my face. With the vibration of the bus the frames keep tapping against the glass. I hear my father sigh with exasperation. All around us people are talking and laughing. The baby stopped crying when the bus started rolling and I imagine him collapsing with relief into his mother's arms. I zero in on the hum of the motor.

When I feel my father elbow me on the side I'm ready to turn around to object and ask him to leave me alone for a while. But when I turn I realize he has accidentally bumped into me as he twisted his body around to talk to the people in the row behind him.

"To Michoacán," I hear him say.

And then a little later, "Oh, that's my son. He goes to college in the United States. He studies letters."

I imagine the people nodding politely, perhaps picturing me hunched over an old book and a magnifying glass, an amplified Cyclops eye scrutinizing the varying lengths of the *l*s, the dissimilar bubble-mouths of the *o*s.

Letters. What had I learned about letters? That they were the building blocks of words that went unspoken, of words that were hurtful, of words that became worthless.

Apá, I have called my father since I was a child. My mother was Mami. I lost both. One to death, one to fear. I have forgiven only one.

No, I have not forgotten my mother, or our relationship through letters.

Just before she became too ill to continue, my mother had been making a concerted effort to master two skills: driving and speaking English. The driving classes were the most difficult because my father was the designated instructor. My father had no patience for such things, which is why I myself didn't get any lessons from him until my sophomore year of high school, the day before I was scheduled to go behind the wheel for driver's ed class. Even then I begged, afraid I'd embarrass myself (which I did anyway) in front of the instructor and the other students. My father agreed to take me out to maneuver through the back roads a few evenings and whenever he slammed his fist against the dashboard I had flashbacks of his teaching technique with my mother.

My mother was more emotional about my father's firm instructions, which became repeated in a severe tone when she failed to follow them to his liking.

"Turn the wheel, Avelina!" he yelled. "Turn the goddamn wheel!"

Of course I had the pressure of driver's ed the week of my lessons and had to pick up the ability quickly, but my mother simply wanted to keep up with my aunts, who were also learning how to drive. Everyone knew that since we were all single-vehicle households, the chances of the women taking possession of the car were nil. Learning to drive was a symbolic gesture of assimilation into this country we had all migrated to where women also drove, to the frustration of my father, who claimed women were nothing more than road hazards. When my father scolded my mother she would push on the breaks, forcing the car to a stop, and then she'd fall over the steering wheel to cry. My brother and I had to observe silently in the back seat under the threat of a knock on the skull if we distracted either the instructor or the student.

I was saddened by my mother's sense of helplessness because I knew she was trying her best. It was my father who made no effort to be patient, or to at least recognize that my mother was capable if not able. My father didn't necessarily subscribe to the stereotypical sexist notions of the Mexican male, but he was somewhat of a stereotype himself: he drank, stayed out late, and came home penniless, the sullen drunk, to ask for my mother's forgiveness. My mother could have taken advantage of his vulnerability but she didn't, which always surprised me. Like the good suffering wife, she forgave him. Perhaps this was why my father's sensibilities didn't soften when he took my mother out for instruction. Not only was he missing out on beer time with his buddies, he was also entertaining my mother's crazy notion about becoming just another woman driver.

I knew about my mother's will to learn because of her second endeavor. Since she had enrolled in night school, taking English classes at the elementary school I attended during the day, I was forced to go with her. For the longest time I didn't understand why since she only had to walk across the street. Years later I realized I was chaperoning, another one of my mother's self-imposed rules, since she was stepping out of the house in the evenings without her husband. I didn't know about such codes of conduct until my female cousin was in her teens and every time she went out on a date, my aunt would force one of her youngest sons to tag along. I also remember my many visits to my grandparents in México, and how my grandmother insisted on leaving the front door ajar and sitting within earshot whenever the young women from the neighborhood, my old childhood friends, came over to chat.

At night school, my mother was playful and excited to be among her former coworkers at the fruit and vegetable packinghouse. Since her health had been failing her she had to quit the strenuous shift, so night school was her reunion with familiar faces. The class was predominantly female. A few women dragged along their spouses, who by the second week all agreed to hang out in the parking lot to drink a few beers while their wives were inside taking notes. The instructor was a handsome young man from the community college who sometimes brought in his guitar to teach the women children's songs in English like "Row, Row, Row Your Boat" and "Mary Had a Little Lamb." At this point the men in the parking lot fled altogether, perhaps embarrassed for their wives who were stuttering through nonsense verse. At least that's what I was feeling for my poor mother who I knew had the worst singing voice in the class. She fumbled her way through the lyrics in her telltale choppy accent. But this didn't stop her and I admired that eventually. The English instructor was instrumental in improving my mother's courage because he was everything my mother's driving instructor was not: he was kind, he didn't raise his voice, and he avoided pointing out his students' weaknesses.

Usually I didn't sit next to my mother during these sessions. Since there were other kids forced by their mothers to come along, we had an instant community and we wandered around the classroom or close by in the schoolyard. We ran around until we heard the desk chairs grating against the floor, signaling the end of the lesson for another week.

My mother, I noticed, was extremely taken by the teacher and tried hard to please him. She made an effort to go up to him at the end of class to show him her work in the bright orange spiral notebook from Pick 'n Save. Yes, she had been practicing both her letters and her words. My mother, I discovered, was only functionally literate. She had not completed the third grade in México. Neither had my father. But even at this my father took a lead since his writing was easier to read than my mother's. My mother wrote very slowly, with a deliberate calculation meant to disguise the fact that she could barely write. When she wanted to correspond with her mother in México, my mother would dictate the letters to me. When my grandmother responded, I had to read the letter back to my mother. Each time the handwriting on my grandmother's letters was different because I knew she had dictated them to one of various school children in her block. My mother used the explanation that she wanted me to practice my Spanish when she asked me to mediate in these matters. My grandmother, I knew, had her own method of hiding the truth of her illiteracy, announcing to everyone that she was nearly blind even though we'd all see her knitting for hours in the afternoons every day of her life. When my mother opted to write an entire letter herself, the process was a long-term commitment, much like the illustrated magazine dramas she kept on the nightstand next to her bed—always the same one for a period of weeks. I could read through one of those, and I usually did, in fifteen minutes. But I never told her that.

As I nod off to sleep on this first afternoon on the road to Michoacán, I promise myself that I will try harder at communicating with my father the next day. Promises are so easy to make in a warm bus steadily approaching the falling night. My grandmother used to say that in order to remember a thought, she had to go back to the place where that thought was originally conceived because place triggers her memory. By dawn the bus will be in a different town—a different state altogether, in fact. Tracing the promise back to its source will be impossible. My father and I are both headed forward, at the same speed for a change. And yet, we continue to go our separate ways.

*O*n the first night on the road I sleep with my head against the window and when I'm not sleeping I nod off from drowsiness, my head thumping against the glass. At the front of the bus, staring out like a clock in a clinic waiting room, is a speedometer that marks up to eighty kilometers per hour. Whenever the bus surpasses that speed an alarm goes off, alerting not only the driver but also the sleeping passengers. All night the goddamned alarm rings, disturbing any peace that might have crept up on us during the dead hours of the night. Reports of devastating bus plunges begin to circle in my head. I've seen enough photographs in the sensationalistic papers *¡Alerta!* and *¡Alarma!* that glare out with bright yellows and reds from every newsstand in Mexicali. These reports come with very little text and an abundance of photographs because showing is more efficiently graphic than telling.

I'm exhausted the next morning, my neck and shoulders sore and stiff. I'm in no mood to face a crowded bus already buzzing with talk. The driver has the radio on low but it's still irritatingly audible. Throughout the night I sucked some of the music into my dreams and the song lyrics reverberated out of the mouths of people I knew. The juxtaposition was surreal and disturbing, like dubbed foreign films where the voices don't quite match the faces on the screen.

I have no idea about any of these small towns the bus drives through, but I deduce the name of the state by the political candidate flyers and posters nailed to the light posts or glued to the murals along the highways. The PAN and PRI parties dominate the publicity overkill. Faces smile amiably, declaring themselves the worthy leaders. Their names and photographs are the only differences from the posters of the last election year's candidates who had affirmed the same thing. I imagine there must be a master plate on file at the party headquarters. This group of bureaucrats lobbies for political seats in Sonora.

The bus stops do not last very long, but there are plenty of them. Every time I see a road sign announcing a new town I brace myself for another fifteen minutes of staring out at the gritty terminals and taking in the chaos of exchanging passengers.

"Do you want a juice or something, you?" my father always asks. No matter what my answer is we both climb down every now and then to stretch. I'm embarrassed for the people who come up to me with crocodile tears to beg for money, their performances unconvincing. I stare at them with disdain. Confronted with this look they go away.

"No need to be nasty," my father says when he catches me in the act.

I roll my eyes. The beggars aren't worth a fight, I think. And then I catch myself at the arrogance my father just pointed out.

When the bus heads south on the road again, exiting the unexciting state of Sonora and entering the state of Sinaloa, it takes a few hours before the landscape changes from a desert to a coast. The waters of the Pacific Ocean are turbulent and I recall the many summers the roads and train tracks were closed because of hurricane damage. I'm upset that I can't hear the breaking of the waves so I attempt to open the window again without success. My father pretends not to notice, even after I glare at him.

"You can help, you," I say. He makes a feeble attempt.

"It's sealed shut," he says. "Look at the lining."

The lining is made of thick, plastic glue, plaster-colored. I look around and realize our window is the only one with this feature.

A few minutes later my father tries to drum up a conversation.

"So when do you finish your career there in college?" he asks.

I take a deep breath. "That depends," I say.

"On what?" he asks.

"Well, many things," I say, not sure about what I'm going to tell him. I had just completed my sophomore year and had declared a vague major in the humanities with an emphasis in creative writing, but friends kept telling me that didn't lead to any kind of job, except maybe teaching. When they suggested I also take up a minor, I thought about a possible minor in French and this didn't elicit much of a hopeful response either.

"Well, it depends on whether I want to be an elementary school teacher, a high school teacher, or a university teacher," I finally say because it sounds thought-out.

"And which do you want to be?" he asks.

"I'm not sure yet," I say, honestly this time. "At this point I just need to complete my degree. By then I'll know."

"That's good, you," he says, and then withdraws into silence. He feigns interest as unconvincingly as I fake politeness.

At the moment I'm especially crabby because my back aches, my ass is numb, and my own smell disgusts me—especially my hands. When I stepped in to use the bathroom at the last terminal I came out draped in its odor of piss. The water I used to wash my hands left them sticky.

"Did I ever tell you the time I got lucky during a holdup on a bus?" my father asks.

I want to tell him the truth. Yes, I know this story. He's told it to me at least three times, and each time he tells it he remembers more details. That's how my father lies, convincing himself more and more that what he's telling is fact, because fiction isn't this exact and memorable.

"I was sitting in the back of the bus on a long trip down to Michoacán," my father begins his implausible tale.

He's sitting in the back of the bus, exhausted into sleep, and his body is slumped down against the window. A hand shakes him awake and he's startled to discover a police officer standing over him.

"Have you been sitting here the entire time?" the officer asks him.

My father, drowsy and confused, says, "Yes, I'm on my way to Michoacán. Are we there yet? What's happened?"

The police officer, a fat man with a mustache, looks at him suspiciously. And then he makes an odd request. "Stay there," he says. "Exactly as you were when you were sleeping."

My father slumps down on his seat again. The police officer takes a few steps back and then, after assessing the situation, steps forward again, shaking his head.

"Mister," the police officer tells him, "you're one lucky cabrón. You just slept through a pinche bus robbery."

My father quickly gets up off his seat and surveys the scene in front of him: weeping women and scared passengers, suitcases and bags emptied out, and a driver with a compress against his face. My father has escaped notice because he is so short and his sleep so deep that he blocks all noises out. No one, the police officer confirms, could see him back there, all alone and lost in the safety of his dreams.

"Can you imagine that?" my father asks me.

"Not really," I say.

"What?" my father says, startled by my response.

"You're short all right. And you sleep like a rock. But you snore like a bull. The robbers would have heard you long before they even climbed on the bus."

My father dismisses my response with his usual nervous laugh. And knowing that nothing will change this mood I'm in, he quickly shifts his attention to those around him on the bus. He's already friendly with the people across the aisle, with the couple sitting behind us, and with the guy seated behind the couple so that he really has to twist his body around to let his voice reach back. Eventually, others on the bus begin to eavesdrop on my father's conversations, which are entertaining to them. My father's contagious laughter makes him the much-appreciated center of attention. An older woman two seats up offers to share her snacks with him. The two guys in the back prod him to join their friendly games of poker. He refuses the invitations, but I know it's a matter of time before he gives in. People keep demanding his attention. *Rigoberto, Rigoberto,*

31

they insist, and the more they say it the more the name becomes exclusively my father's and no longer mine. Slowly I'm becoming silent and invisible, the overlooked companion to my father.

By noon the bus driver makes a break for lunch. When the bus pulls over I don't want to get off because the smell of food at that moment will turn my stomach. I remain in my seat, grateful for the privacy, away from my father's booming voice and popularity. I watch from the window as he plays cards over a basket of fried chicken with the two guys from the back of the bus. One of them calls himself Zacatecas.

Only two other passengers remain on the bus with me. I can hear the man's shaky voice in the back. "To the bathroom, Mama?" he says. His mother responds with a guttural sound. The man lifts the old woman and strains to fit her into the cramped stall. With the door wide open, the stench of urine immediately spreads through the cabin. I pinch my nose. The old woman's eyes remain shut the entire time.

"Knock, Mama. Knock when you're done," he says after he has placed her in the stall and shut the door. He looks over at me. I smile, hoping he will know that I understand about sick mothers.

"Is that your father traveling with you?" he asks, coming a few rows forward. He's balding, but I can't gauge his age.

Startled, I stammer a yes.

"I thought he was your brother," he says, smiling.

I chuckle weakly, accepting his compliment on my father's behalf. I have my father's name but look nothing like him. I'm taller and wear glasses; he's much darker, with curly hair and straight teeth. There's no reason for anyone to suspect we're related, sitting side by side on a bus that switches passengers at every terminal. Besides, we have been speaking very little to each other. I do hope, however, that I will inherit my father's slow aging. This is not the first time someone has pointed out how young my father looks. And although no one says it, I know they're also impressed by how handsome he is. My brother and I are round-faced and soft-featured, like our mother was.

"That's my mother in there, you know," he says. "My brother got out of the bus to eat. We're taking turns. We're bringing her back to Sinaloa. Where are you headed?"

"Michoacán," I answer.

"It's a longer journey than ours," he says.

When I don't keep the dialogue going he continues.

"She's sick, you know, and we can't take care of her anymore. It's for the best. We love her very much, you know."

At that moment we both feel awkward, but we're spared from further embarrassment by the feeble knocking behind the bathroom door.

"I hear you, Mama," he calls back. He bows his head. "Nice talking to you," he says, then rushes back unnecessarily since the bathroom is located only a few seats behind him.

Passengers begin to climb back on the bus after half an hour. My father brings me a cold pint of orange juice and a fried chicken leg I eventually consume, surprised at how hungry I really am. And suddenly I'm aware at how comfortable I accept my father's newfound paternal role—feeding me as if I were still a child. As I eat I think about the man with his mother. He's suffering from what my grandmother calls *cabeza llena*—a mind so full with thinking, that he has to let some words leak out or the brain will implode. *Desahogarse*, she calls that process. Letting things out to unburden the head. Holding your breath too long can suffocate you. When the bus reaches the next station, the bald man carries his mother off while she sleeps. He moves her without her knowing, and I imagine her waking up in some room, with an unfamiliar face standing over her, trying to calm her down with a soothing but strange voice. I feel bad for both of them. When he walks past me, he doesn't even turn his head to nod good-bye.

In the long stretch of road that follows, the bus is uncharacteristically silent. Perhaps the post-nourishment exhaustion has finally settled. Since no one else seems interested in talking, my father sets his sights on me. I feel oddly grateful.

33

"You know what I always wanted to be?" my father says.

I shrug my shoulders.

"An electrician," he says.

"Don't you know something about that already?" I ask. I remember that he used to tinker with wires and fuse boxes, like my aunt's husband who was a licensed electrician in Mexicali before he moved to the United States and became a maintenance worker at the golf courses in Palm Springs.

"Just things I picked up when I was about your age, no, maybe younger than you," he says. "I was apprenticed to an electrician for a while, but then I left it."

"What happened?" I ask.

"Your grandfather didn't think that would lead to anything. Not like being a farmworker."

When he says this I sense the bitter taste in his mouth. His eyes gaze out sadly as if he's looking at the day my grandfather made the decision to take him out of the electrical shop and push him into the fields. I feel a heavy weight in my chest for him, and I rack my mind in search of the right words to offer him—words that don't sound sarcastic or cruel, but words that can touch him as delicately as he touched me with his admission. But I can't think of anything so I stay quiet. And it's in that moment that all of our luck changes because the bus breaks down at the Sinaloa-Nayarit border.

An hour into the delay, passengers grumble as the cabin succumbs quickly to the humidity. I run my finger across the dusty glass, my buttocks sore from lack of circulation. A stream of sweat slides down my spine and it would have driven me to madness had I not found humor in the bus driver's request for volunteers to help push the bus down the road.

"Just over the hump," he says. "It'll roll down on its own from there."

My father is the first to volunteer. I shake my head.

"Zacatecas!" he calls to one of his poker buddies in the back. Zacatecas joins him, as do a number of the other men on board.

34

When I don't budge from my seat I become ashamed at the realization that no one has expected me to help. I hear my father take the lead, giving directions, suggestions, and an occasional word of encouragement. The crew manages to shove the bus over the hump, and then it coasts to the side of the road where it sits for the rest of the day until a mechanic arrives. The mechanic tinkers with the engine all afternoon and into the evening. The passengers scatter on the ground, seeking shelter from the sweltering heat beneath trees and in a nearby roadside restaurant whose owner beams at his unexpected fortune. I stand at a distance, observing as my father and the rest of the clientele darken into shadows with the passing of the hours. In time a second bus arrives and we all transfer our luggage over. As we drive off, the mechanic seems unfazed by his defeat, watching us pull into the road, a bottle of beer in his hand, which he raises toward us as a sign of farewell.

My father avoids eye contact at this point as if he's expecting me to gripe about the second-class bus ride once again, but I don't. I'm too worn out to complain. When he turns his head away from me, I know he's trying to hide the smell of alcohol in his breath. I roll over in my seat and try to sleep as well.

"I know I shouldn't be drinking," he says in a low voice.

I have heard these words many times before.

"Do you know what I want more than anything in the entire world, you?"

Silence.

"I want you to be happy. You're too depressed. I want to see you smile. You have your mother's smile. Why don't you show it to me?"

No response.

"Do you know what I want more than anything in the entire world, you?" he says again. He struggles to keep his eyes open, so I stay quiet and let him fall asleep.

"Are you asleep, you?" I whisper to my father. He doesn't move but he breathes heavily. When he begins to snore I know he's out. I look around. The entire cabin seems to be lost in deep sleep.

I push his body to the other side and shift his head to quiet down his snoring. I had seen my mother do this a number of times when she helped him into bed. I imagine his second wife has learned this trick by now.

Once his body seems comfortable and at peace, I relax. This bus is in better shape and drives more smoothly. I crack open the window to let the air in. When I start dozing off I attempt to match my father's breathing rhythm but can't. My body trembles as I lean on him. I'm lulled by the steady rise and fall of his body. I want to remain attached to him this way all night. When I begin to sniffle, a thin tear making its way weakly down my cheek, my father awakes with a start and pushes his body against mine before quickly falling asleep again. I can't tell if this is an accidental shove, or if it's his way of telling me to stop, that the other passengers on the bus might hear me crying in the dark. I shift my body toward the warm metal of the bus, my knee pressed painfully against the armrest, away from my father.

When I wake up during the still hours of the early morning my father is gone, probably to the toilet. Still, the empty seat saddens me because it holds the memory of my father's body.

Or is it, I fear to admit, my lover's body I yearn for? I want to wear the weight of him like armor. My lips tremble at the thought of him roaming the college campus for his next conquest, keeping watch for the timid young man who shies away from the cafeteria tables that are too crowded or too loud. He will seek him out, the one with the vulnerable eyes. The poetry of his seduction is irresistible. And the stupid young man will let him sit next to him and never leave, not even when the boyfriend kicks his shin beneath the all-concealing table cloths at fancy restaurants he'd never afford with his student budget. But he will learn about wines, Italian desserts, and condiments so tasty and exotic they're like portholes into other parts of the world. But there will also be the backhand to the chest on the car ride home, and the painful words: *stupid ignorant farmworker, dumb-ass sissy greaser, beaner cunt.* And at night he will reel himself back into favor by appealing to the young man's most sensitive part of his soul—his memory.

"Cuéntame más de tu padre," my lover will request in the young man's native tongue. And the stupid young man will comply because Spanish is his weakness and because the only muscles that can move in post-rapture are thought and pain and voice.

Cuéntame más de tu amante, my longing demands, and I want to tell it all. I want to tell it all to my father. Not to antagonize him further, or to hurt him, but to let him know I have learned about love and loss, and that this brings us closer together than the shared grief of the death of my mother, the death of his wife.

Listen to this, Apá: in May of 1989, seven months after leaving home, I met a man twenty years my senior. He was a man whose eyes were like rooms with the lights always on, and he said he had much to show me. He touched every part of my body with the tip of his tongue because I had the softest skin he had ever felt on either man or woman. "Like an eternity without speed bumps," he said as his fingers glided from my thigh to my spine and over my shoulder to my chest. He wanted to claim every inch of me, and when all of me was his he wanted more. So I gave him my stories as well. He wanted every story, every name and place and piece of gossip. I gave it to him. I gave because he was an excellent listener, and because sometimes his ability to put the past into words didn't work. And when he couldn't explain himself he hurt me. So there I was, using the gift that you and I have been given, el don del cuento, to ward off my lover's wrath.

When my father returns from the toilet, he notices the angst on my face. He tussles my hair.

"Are you getting anxious?" he asks.

"A little," I say.

"Tell me—" we both say at once, and let out a laugh together.

"You tell me first," he insists, even though he's the superior storyteller.

Ghost Whisper to My Lover

Tell you something else about my father? Claro, querido.

*My father holds a peculiar fascination for extraterrestrial life. He was pleased to discover that a magazine existed for people like him, the Spanish version of UFO—*OVNI: Objetos voladores no identificados, *which came packed with firsthand narrative accounts of close encounters with space aliens. He sought out the magazine for years even though his reading skills weren't very strong, but it didn't matter since the stories came fully illustrated with amateur drawings depicting these intriguing and evasive creatures.*

In the afternoons when he came home from work he parked the car behind the back porch since only my grandfather was allowed to park in front. When he wasn't having a beer with my uncle after dinner, he liked to stand against the car through the evenings and look up at the stars. I never got tired of him pointing out Polaris. I pretended to be surprised each time. And on one occasion he confessed to me that one of his fantasies was to be abducted by a UFO.

"For what?" I asked, shuddering at the idea of space travel. At the time, our favorite show was Battlestar Galactica. *Our favorite reruns:* Star Trek *and the black-and-white* Twilight Zone *and* Outer Limits *episodes. But I suspected that the imagination of special effects and costume artistry did not even begin to address the disconcerting reality of what was out there.*

"Just," he responded quizzically. "Just to know."

I didn't ask what it was exactly he wanted to know. I simply gazed up at the stars with him and tried to imagine the extraterrestrial forces that had mesmerized my father so much he wanted to become part of it. I also suspect he has kept his fantasy alive after all these years, even if tucked safely in his house, his weary eye catching a glimpse at the evening sky from his living room or the kitchen as the day comes to a close and his mind escapes however briefly from the turmoil of worries and responsibilities. My father, the farmworker and cosmonaut, floats out into space with his back turned to the world, his face looking fearlessly into the great abyss of things mysterious, unknown, and new.

Childhood
and Other
Language Lessons

Bakersfield, California, 1970–72

My father gave up boxing a few years before I was born. According to my mother's sisters he wasn't a very good contender anyway. Their assessment was based entirely on the only match they ever saw him fight. This was also his last match. His humiliation at being knocked out seconds after the first-round bell was so great that he never returned to the boxing ring. My aunts wouldn't let him forget the day he had wanted to impress my mother's family and they lorded this failure over him as a tactic to keep him from coming around to ask for my mother in the evenings.

"You should have seen your father," my aunt once told me, pleased that she could keep this story fresh after all these years. "He barely had time to lift his glove when his opponent floored him with a right hook. Even the referee thought it was a joke and nudged him with his foot before he realized he should start counting. Isn't that right, you?" My father grinned sheepishly from the corner.

My father's post-boxer years are the beginning of my story.

Since no level of ridicule could keep him away from my mother, my father continued to court her. On their dates they had to take a chaperone, usually one of my mother's sisters, who had to bring back a full report to my grandmother to insure the honesty of his intentions. But my father suspected that my grandmother and aunts were scheming to break up the relationship. My grandmother wasn't too keen about having her oldest child marry a farmworker/defeated boxer, and a probable drunk to boot. Wasn't he a bit quick to accept an offer for a drink? And what of those awful tattoos? Had he needled them in himself? So my father, out of desperation, did what any young man from Zacapu, Michoacán would do in a situation like this: he skipped town with his girlfriend.

My parents eloped the summer of 1969, leaving Michoacán behind and shacking up in an avocado-colored one-room house in Mexicali, where they planned my mother's crossing into California. My father had his work permit, so he crossed the international border every day to work the fields of the Imperial Valley, usually picking beets. Every paycheck brought him one step closer to earning the fee for borrowing a passport for my mother. In front of the house grew a dwarf palm, across the street stood a bakery, and across the international border awaited the promise of a better life. The goal grew in urgency once my mother realized early the following year that she was pregnant.

As my father tells it, by the middle of spring my paternal grandparents were already following the grape route north into central California, but my mother had reservations about joining them since she wanted to start a family independently of her in-laws. My father convinced her that there was safety in numbers and that they should live near family, especially in a foreign country. So before my mother became too big to travel they crossed over using a borrowed local passport for my mother and once it was returned, favor paid for, they simply drove north, past the Coachella Valley, past Los Angeles, and into the county of Kern. When night fell they took to driving through the back roads because the highways and the speeding cars with their maddening bright lights frightened my mother. They came across a fork.

"Which way should we go, you?" my father asked my mother.

My mother contemplated the two paths before them for a few seconds. The roads were dark and neither gave any hint about where it was heading. My mother said that it really didn't matter. Both roads were going north. Since she was pregnant and an undocumented alien, she only wanted to make sure that her child was born a U.S. citizen. Any city would do.

"Which way then, Avelina?" my father pressed on.

"Go right," my mother said, pointing. And right they turned, arriving in Bakersfield, California, where I was born on July 18, 1970, and where my brother, Alexandro, was born almost two years later, on March 27, 1972.

My parents carried very few things with them during that crossing, but among them were the boxing gloves and shorts, the memorabilia of my father's bachelor years. In the old family albums there's a photograph that shows me trying them on for size. The shorts reach down to my ankles, and the gloves are so heavy that my father needs to hold my wrists up so that I can pose like a true champion. Behind us, the corner of a cradle is just visible, and over the cradle is my mother's shadow keeping watch over my newborn baby brother—keeping watch over all three of us, in fact, since it must have been for her amusement that my father dressed me up in his pugilist's garb.

The stay in Bakersfield was brief. Everyone had a different answer to the question: Why did we return to Zacapu in the summer of 1972? My grandmother said that my parents wanted to make peace with my mother's family, and that there was no better peace offering than a pair of rambunctious boys—the first grandchildren. My grandfather said that the family thought it was time to make use of that old house in Colonia Miguel Hidalgo that was being constructed the entire time they worked the grapes in Delano, Lamont, and Bakersfield, and what better time than in the middle of all this César Chávez-inspired strike-and-boycott furor. My father said that he and my uncle were afraid of that Viet Nam draft that kept plundering the fields of young men. My uncle said that they had misread some notification about the expiration of their work permits, but instead of researching a renewal, my father had gotten all worked up about using their savings to buy musical equipment, start a band, and live off paying gigs for a change instead of picking grapes. My mother said that all of those reasons were true, but that there were a few more. And that eventually I'd be old enough to know and understand them.

Zacapu, México, 1972–79

We descended on a half-completed corner building in Colonia Miguel Hidalgo. Miguel Hidalgo y Costilla had been the priest who in 1810 stirred the Mexican people into action, which eventually lead to México's independence from Spain in 1821—300 years after the conquest of Hernán Cortés over the Aztec empire. México had one long history of battles and it seemed appropriate that los González arrive to start some trouble of their own.

The construction of the second story of our house had been halted by a lack of funds but the ground floor was complete enough to inhabit. On the top floor we kept the dogs that barked incessantly at passersby through the ghost windows. The eight rooms below were purpose-shifters, always changing function. One year's kitchen became next year's living room. A bedroom became a rented storage space for the corn harvested in the field behind our house. Once, my grandfather briefly ran a small bodega from one of the rooms. The Pepsi logo outside the service window was still visible for years after it had been painted over. The main dining room became my father's rehearsal studio when he had his short-lived band. Although it had undergone a number of transformations over the years, the house always had the nicest garden in the block. My grandparents have always been skilled gardeners, and they successfully grew everything from medicinal herbs to papaya plants, from chile habanero to figs.

At one time they even kept a talking parrot that made its home in the lime tree. This pet was the cause of my mother's consternation for months because my uncles had only taught it to cuss. The bird spewed out obscenities at every unsuspecting visitor. It never discriminated, squawking out *¡Chinga tu madre!* at the neighborhood drunk with the same conviction as the insults he swore to our teacher-nuns from the parochial school, coming by to collect the monthly tuition. It took a stone's throw from a furious passerby to silence the bird forever.

As a reminder of my family's failed enterprise, the outdoor cement stairs led the way to the unfinished second floor where the dogs with an irrepressible hatred for strangers watched over us. This house was my world. My world was Zacapu—the place of my father's birth. His mother, a full-blooded Purépecha Indian, had been born in nearby Nahuatzen. My mother and her father were born in nearby Janamuato. Her mother was born in nearby Morelia. Only my father's father had been born outside of the country, in the north, like I had been.

In Zacapu (once Tzacapu) we also had the beauty of the surrounding mountains and not far off the enchanting Lago de Pátzcuaro, where Janitzio salutes from the center with its giant statue of José María Morelos y Pavón, the other famous Mexican priest who led the independence movement after the execution of Miguel Hidalgo y Costilla. The name of our town comes from the Nahautl word for rock, but the area was actually lush with the lumber-producing pino, encino, madroño, and to a lesser extent, tocuz and capiz trees. The greenery was ripe with apple, capulín, membrillo, zapote, and avocado trees. In the fields, corn and coffee were abundant. Much later I learned that the farmers were replacing the old crops on the fertile hills with the more profitable marijuana planted by the acres. And nearby was Anguangueo, the famous monarch butterfly sanctuary, where the fiery invasions took place in early springs. We'd walk around wearing butterflies like appliqués on our clothing. And when they fluttered by the dozens so close to the ground, I'd run through the sea of them, disappearing behind the bursts of light coming through their wings. I have never come across such intensity of breath and beauty since, and when I see a monarch pictured in a magazine or television screen I'm swept back into the strange but comforting intimacy of their winking paradise. I tried many times to claim a snippet of this spectacle by hiding a monarch in my pocket, hoping I could recreate the marvelous sputter in the privacy of my room. But all I ever pulled out was the orange-black powder of the crushed insect, and the specks of debris evoked nothing of its original shape.

In the summers, my father hunted for wild fowl, squirrel, and hare, carrying my younger brother with him in a knapsack. I complained about the long walks but I was too heavy to carry on his back, so he left me at home most of the time. I didn't object. I had already been through too many ordeals up in the mountains.

Once I had been following a string of three hunters at night, my father in front of the line. I lagged behind because the three men carried miner helmets with lights that illuminated my path. Since it was the rainy season, the marshes grew out and the grasses covering the waters had softened. As we trudged along my legs submerged up to the ankles in the soggy soil, making sucking sounds each time I raised my feet to take the next step. The slingshot in my back pocket kept digging into my buttocks and I remembered with much guilt all of the lizards I had decapitated or disemboweled with my cruel aim. All of a sudden my foot sank knee-deep into a hole. I let out a scream and this aroused quick action from the men, who all turned to face me, their lights shining down on my body. I looked down. The hole was a nest of water snakes and the disturbed hatchlings twisted wildly around my leg as I imagined that the severed lizard tails had come back to seek vengeance. I must have jumped like a frightened cat because in the next moment I was out of the hole and skipping my way out of the marsh. My father's laughter echoed behind me.

My most fearful moments on the mountain seemed to amuse my father, who was more than willing to embellish the details as he told the stories repeatedly. I became resentful. I never forgave him for the day he made me ride a donkey up to the mountain by myself. He met up with a friend who was going up for firewood, the long-eared beast at his side. I heard them discuss how intelligent these animals were, that they were able to memorize paths and retrace them at their master's bidding. To prove this point, the men put me on the donkey's back and gave it a swift slap on the ass. Cold with fear, I rode nearly lying down as the donkey galloped at a steady speed, finally coming to a halt when it reached a small cabin a long way into the woods. My father and his friends found me there some time later, still grasping the donkey's stringy mane.

That same evening he put me on a makeshift swing—a log with a rope tied around its middle, the other end thrown over the high branch of a tree. He made me sit on the log with the knot at my crotch. He then pulled the other end of the rope to lift me like a swinging piñata in the air. The more I cried the more he pulled on the rope, as if he were pushing my lack of bravado further away from him and his friends. I realized that time that my father was intoxicated, that going hunting up to the mountains was his way of hiding his drinking from my mother.

"I'm going to tell Mami!" I threatened out of desperation. This only fueled the laughter.

"I'm going to tell her you were drunk!"

A silence fell on the revelers. When I began to descend I knew that I'd found a way to keep my father in line. The log reached the ground and I fell to my knees, my legs too weak to prop me up. I saw my father release the end of the rope and walk away without saying a word. When we returned home, I didn't mention any of what had happened to my mother. In fact, I realized that my mother already knew what went on during these hunting expeditions. Her stoic reception of my father's kill said it all.

At about this time I began to recognize the signs of bad things to come. My father began drinking more heavily. Dinastía, the fantasy musical venture, fell to the wayside; the sound equipment was sold. My paternal grandparents returned to the United States, followed shortly by my uncle and his family. Only my parents were left behind to look after the house and share babysitting duties.

My father was expected to look after my brother and me when my mother went shopping or went to church with my maternal grandmother. He wasn't very dedicated to the task. As soon as my mother was out of sight he found his way to Zuniga's Bar at the end of the street. Since he could see us from the stool at the bar, he probably deduced he was technically still keeping an eye on things.

One afternoon I tired of running around in the street and stuffing my face with candies I bought with the money my father gave me before he entered the bar. I went inside to catch my favorite cartoon, *Archie and Friends.* My brother preferred to stay outside, riding his squeaky bicycle up and down the cobblestone street. As soon as I turned on the television I was excited to find out the program was just beginning. The opening tune was a familiar one, with Archie and gang playing in their band. I became so wound up I decided to jump from my mother's vanity table to the bed and then back again. I did so repeatedly and with so much success that I became overconfident, paying closer attention to the cartoon. Distracted, I miscalculated a leap and struck my head on the corner of the wooden table, breaking open my skin at the eyebrow. I felt the blood gushing out quickly. A piece of toilet paper wasn't enough to stop the flow, neither was one of the kitchen towels. I panicked. Through the garden fence I waved at my brother for help, my face watery with tears and blood.

"What happened?" my brother asked, rushing over for a close look.

I burst out into uncontrollable sobs. "Get Papi," I demanded.

Before running out to the bar, he came inside and brought me the entire roll of toilet paper, which he pressed against my forehead. The roll dampened soon enough.

As I waited for my father to arrive I anticipated the beating I was about to get. But when he finally came he was more panic-struck than I was. Tipsy, he tried to stop the bleeding but nothing worked. I was too relieved about not getting punished to worry about the visit to the Red Cross, the stitches, or my mother's anger at my father when she returned later in the afternoon. My maternal grandmother also came over to have to her say.

"You useless drunk," she scolded my father. "Your son could have bled to death, you!"

That weekend we went out to the movies, a rare family outing we couldn't really afford. I fell asleep in the middle of *Close Encounters of the Third Kind,* waking up when the theater lights went up. I was too drowsy to remember what that patch of gauze was doing stuck to my face.

Soon after that incident my father returned to work in the United States, a birthplace I had no memory of. Most of the house was empty by then, the furniture sold. Only my mother held on to our few belongings, as if keeping at bay the day we would finally have to leave as well. I was very glad when it finally came, because the months before that moment were the days of want.

We were going hungry. A person who experiences hunger never forgets that feeling. It is more than emptiness, more than an ache at the center of the stomach—it is a waking up and going to bed with shame, as if this stiffness of the jaw and hardening of the belly is part of some punishment. The flesh begins to feel transparent, and a strange echo resounds in the room when you admit to your weeping mother that you want real food, not tortilla with cheese and hot sauce, which she's been feeding you the entire month. But my mother insisted on keeping it a secret, even from her family who lived across the main highway in Colonia Obrera, where the town cemetery lay. No one would have thought it possible anyway, since our building had been built on dollars and, filled with all the contemporary furniture, it housed the former musician's family. I felt as vacant as the tears of wax running down the candle lit for the bedside portrait of Jesus. The flame illuminated his Sacred Heart, which was already bursting with rays of light. Jesus looked well fed and healthy—so unlike the rest of us, sallow and sorry-eyed. I would spend the rest of my childhood making up for that empty stomach by overeating—by digesting the memory of hunger.

At night, after slipping a sugar cube into my mouth as she put me to bed, my mother went to her bed to cry. I thought it was because of the sugar cube, a treat I never shared with my brother, who fell asleep sooner than I did. I thought that maybe she'd stop her sobbing if I gave it back to her. But I didn't. I jealously guarded the small rock of sweetness behind my tongue, knowing that if my mother returned to reclaim it I could quickly swallow it.

Into the second month, my mother finally relented and told her parents, who were beside themselves with outrage. They came to the rescue immediately and sent word to my father that my mother was leaving him for abandonment and neglect. I remember finally tasting milk and how the ecstasy of it made me break out into tears.

It was never made clear to me why my father didn't send money the entire time he was gone. Even more confusing was how he had survived his return to Zacapu. Whatever collisions of wrath took place happened offstage. I only remember that my father brought back for me a large bag of candies and that I stuffed myself with sugar all evening, hoarding the sweets beneath my pillow and taking one into my mouth each time I woke up during the night. The next morning I was sick to the point of vomiting, and I recall my grandmother standing over me as I wretched into a bucket. She yelled out to my father, "Even your candy is worthless, you!"

Another migration was imminent. I can only speculate why my mother agreed to the move back to the United States. Perhaps she wanted to save her marriage. Perhaps she wanted to keep my father on a shorter leash. On his own he was undependable and careless with his earnings. In any case, my paternal grandparents came down from California to help convince my mother that the best option was a return to the United States. My Purépecha grandmother was given the task of convincing my brother and me that the move to the north was a good thing. Her selling point was the school lunch.

"They feed you there," she said. "For free."

As for the house in Colonia Hidalgo, it remained an unfinished dream home, the largest structure on the block. The dogs eventually died of sickness or old age and the first floor became as hollow as the second. I last saw the house in 1984 on a trip I took with my grandparents, who arrived in Zacapu that year with the sole purpose of getting rid of it. The house, which had been built on the backs of my grandparents and their children, had lost its charm. The once lush garden had been neglected for years and a broken water pipe flooded the floors, soiling the lower edges of the walls like the corrupted hems of ankle-length dresses. The lonely custodian—an old widow with a severe case of edema—seemed grateful that my grandparents had arrived from the north to relieve her of her duty. She greeted us from the window to the room that used to be mine as a child, and this pained me. Especially since instead of a diaphanous curtain, she had hung a thick wool blanket to help insulate her sleeping quarters, now only a dark shadow of what used to be my private space. The house was no longer my home, and I felt intrusive going in. My grandfather gave her the news of the impending sale, his voice echoing in the empty hall, and we left within minutes, none of us commenting on the mossy smell that had permeated the brick and cement. The loss of this house was the final gesture of good-bye and the clearest evidence that I would never return to live in Michoacán again. But most distressingly, I had lost the first home of my memory yet again.

Thermal, California, 1979—80

My family came to settle in the southern California desert, in the town appropriately named Thermal in the predominantly Mexican Coachella Valley 130 miles south of Los Angeles and 95 miles north of Mexicali and the international border. This town was known as the Grape Capital of the World because of the endless acres of the crop spread across its landscape. The town also conveniently housed many of the farmworkers who worked the maintenance and harvest. My family believed that by moving here we would never run out of work again.

I was born into a culture of work. Since the age of the Bracero Program of the 1940s, the state of Michoacán has been the number one exporter of Mexican farm labor to the United States. It is not out of the ordinary to witness entire communities of farmworkers migrate back and forth between the two countries—an echo of the region's famous monarch butterflies who do the same for survival, their spectacular flights across the continent retraced generations later through genetic memory. When we descended on Thermal, los González were no strangers to dramatic change. We had been moving north and south for four generations, which explains why my great-grandfather and father were Mexican-born citizens, while my grandfather and I were U.S.-born citizens.

And now here we were in Thermal, three generations living under the same roof: my paternal grandparents, all three of their married children plus their bachelor son, and their ten grandchildren. Only my aunt's family came from Mexicali, where her five children had been born. My three older cousins had already completed elementary school and had been enrolled in secondary school in México when they were pulled out. They frequently voiced resentment for the move and never quite adjusted to the United States until they were old enough to marry and settle down many years later.

Despite the communal arrangement, with each family unit contributing to the overall household budget, we still failed to make ends meet at the end of each month. One of the great ironies of southern California is its susceptibility to even mild winters. Winter is a critical period in the lifeline of crops because the orchards and grape fields are maturing in preparation for the spring harvest. A winter in a landscape where temperatures can reach 120 degrees Fahrenheit in the summer is relative and doesn't need to reach a low extreme to damage the tender citrus and grapes, shortening the picking season.

With a body count of eighteen, we lived squeezed into an apartment with four rooms. Clothes and bed sheets were public property and during mealtime the dining room was as mad as a cafeteria, one person looking around for the next available seat, plate in hand. Our extended family was a necessity for socioeconomic livelihood, not a romanticized notion of togetherness and unity; by sticking together there was less of a chance of going hungry. But the compromise was the loss of privacy.

The grandchildren spread out on the living room carpet to sleep at night. Each morning I woke up among contorted bodies pressed against another in an effort to accommodate bent elbows and knees, jigsaw puzzle style. There was only one bathroom, so getting up earlier than anyone else meant no waiting in line with your legs crossed. Females had priority because males could go out back and piss in the brush. Our grandfather showed my boy cousins and me how to do it

56

after he had to give up his turn to my mother. We all stared down at the spots of damp soil behind the van. He pointed.

"See there? For us men the world is our toilet."

Having one bathroom also led to a number of embarrassing encounters. If someone knocked on the door while you were in the shower you had to wrap a towel around you, suds stiffening your hair. And no matter how large the towel, there was still too much exposed flesh. I could have lived without having seen my grandmother's wrinkled cleavage, or my uncle's dark and slightly uneven nipples, or the look of terror in my cousin's eyes as he struggled to conceal his prepubescent erection. Those indiscreet moans and groans escaping through the house at night concretized into the images of skin and coarse hairs. The bras, the panties, the stretched-out underwear waving from the clothesline in the back suddenly claimed their owners. How real my family had become as I witnessed their belching, farting, vomiting, and fucking. Still, I longed for the days my father could afford to pay our own rent. I scavenged for scraps of hope at the crowded dinner table where the adult conversation always centered on paychecks and job prospects. At that time my father and my uncle were unemployed. Our families were feeding off the reluctant generosity of my grandfather, a man so thrifty he would wear a shirt as long as the biggest holes were the ones through which he slipped in his head and arms. Once he even bragged that a white woman saw him walking down the street and stopped her car to hand him a bag with her lunch because she thought he was homeless.

"Dark cookies and a ham sandwich," he replied when someone asked him what was in the bag. "More like dog biscuits and a shoe sole," he added. My youngest cousins giggled.

My grandfather was the man with all the confidence and the money to back it up. My father's was the loudest voice at the table, but my grandfather's was the voice with the fury of a pickaxe. He knew how to chip a person's confidence down to the size of a quarry pebble.

"I think Leonel will talk to his boss about giving me a chance with the tractor," my father said, throwing out a spark of enthusiasm on the dinner table.

"*Leonel?*" my grandfather cried out, incredulously. "That good-for-nothing drunk? A recommendation from him is like telling the boss he wants to take his beer buddy along to keep him company. No, you'll get nowhere with that lazy friend of yours, you."

"Well, if that doesn't work out, there's Sancho—"

"*Sancho?* Are you out of your mind? He's got a callous on his fat ass from sitting around at the unemployment office. They should label a chair for him. That man can't keep a job for a month."

My uncle tried to save the day. "There's always Ricardo."

"*Ricardo?*"

I lost steam much sooner than my father and uncle. I withdrew from the table, defeated. My most intense fantasy at that time was that my grandfather keeled over from a heart attack, making us heirs to his hidden riches. But I suspected that he lived for those tugs-of-war over dinner. Besides, there was not much of an inheritance, only the small stash of savings he kept in a secret pocket on the inside of his belt. (He didn't believe in banks.) My grandmother revealed the hiding place to us in case my grandfather kicked the bucket in the middle of the street. She wanted to make sure the cash didn't drive off with the paramedics.

She warned: "Those people peel off your jewelry and pluck your wallet. And how the hell do you prove it when you're lying there cross-eyed like a billy goat on a puddle of your own drool?"

There were few choice activities for me during the suffocating evenings. Although I had eight cousins (all but two were male) and a brother to play with, I preferred to keep to myself. The boys were gruff and rowdy and spent too many hours exchanging dirty jokes. Riding bikes with them meant parking at the ravine to talk about tits and pussy. Our oldest cousin liked to brag he was the only one who had engaged in sex so he was the designated reader of the text in pornographic magazines. He even mimicked the *ooh*s and *ahh*s. Too bored to bother with my cousin's fake orgasms, I usually hid away in my parents' room, where all our belongings were stored.

In that cramped room there was a permanently sealed door in the wall shared with the apartment next door. The building had apparently been larger at one time, but the owners were making a killing with the division of that one unit into two, both for rent. The unit next door was not even a one-bedroom; it was more like a studio with one common area and a bathroom in the back. I knew about its size because I saw it frequently, through a small hole a few inches from the bottom of the door. The hole was small enough to fit a cable or telephone wire through, but now it was just my peephole. I had come across it by accident one afternoon after I decided to imitate my older female cousin who hid beneath her mother's bed to nap. She slept undisturbed and undiscovered by our grandfather, who detested finding anyone sleeping during the daytime. He said this was a sign of laziness. No one mentioned the fact that he himself napped in the afternoons, and he may have thought that none of us knew, but we could hear him snoring even with his room sealed shut.

In the long lean months we lived there I saw plenty of the occupants next door. My method was simple: I lay down next to the bed, ready to roll behind the edge of the comforter in case either of my parents walked in. The light seeping in through the hole guided my curious eye.

I knew nothing more gratifying than learning about people who didn't know I was watching. It was better than the school experiment of growing a potato plant in a cup of water. These were the people from the other side of the wall, not the dull, food stamp clan from this side. Exciting things happened over there, not here in the place of mismatched socks and plastic spoons that got washed for reuse. Another world spun into existence, and it was a little bit mine as well.

Once there were four women in their twenties sharing the rent next door. They worked at the vegetable packinghouse with my mother and my aunts. My cousins whistled at them when they walked by; my oldest cousin claimed he had fucked one of them.

Little did they know that in the mornings the women walked around in pantyhose, comfortable in their bare breasts. The curly-haired woman always sat on a cot against the opposite wall to apply her lipstick. She was the plain one, refusing to wear miniskirts and tube tops like the other women. On weekend evenings she stayed behind, watching from the cot as the others dressed up for a night out. When they left, she secured the door and then proceeded to look through her roommates' belongings. She never took anything; she simply held and touched, clasping her fingers around barrettes, combs, and an assortment of makeup kits. I watched her empty out entire bags and shoe boxes over her cot, only to take her time putting back the contents, sometimes sniffing the powders or rubbing the smooth plastics against her cheeks. Once she was bent over the cot and I zeroed in on a small bow in the center of her panties. The bow was tearing off, crooked, and the white flesh of her buttocks showed through the opening. I immediately shut my eyes and turned my head in shame, though that image haunted me for days. When the lights went off, the bow glowed in the dark of my mind. Each time I felt the urge to cry.

The four women moved out after just a few months, but the unit didn't remain empty for long. A married couple with an infant child moved in. We heard them argue and throw things against the wall at all hours of the day. The infant's bellowing added to the chaos. The couple called each other names back and forth until the man beat his wife and the room quieted down to a muffled whimpering. My mother was fed up with these daily episodes so she urged my father to speak with the neighbor. He took my uncle with him.

"So we told the guy it wasn't our business or anything like that," my father reported over dinner, "but that he should be discreet about his ways."

My grandfather only nodded in silence. That was one of the few instances he kept his mouth shut, refusing to volunteer an opinion. The common knowledge that he beat my grandmother was left unspoken, yet it might as well have been announced by the way the dining room went dead silent.

I never saw the couple's heads because they had propped a table against the sealed door. I could only see their legs—one pair following the second from one side of the room to the other. It was like watching leopards pace left and right in a cage at the zoo, felines bored to frustration. The man once pulled up a chair to the table and sat down in the buff. His shriveled cock looked down at me. It was a sad and delicate appendage, timid. It was the first adult man's penis I had ever seen that wasn't a photograph or a caricature. It looked nothing like the large erect ones in my cousin's porno magazines. This penis was pale and stubby. So powerless, it didn't seem like much at all. I became embarrassed for the man, and the shame of having seen him in such a vulnerable state kept me away from the peephole until the next tenant.

The new tenant was an older white man with few possessions: a dusty bed, a chair, a tattered suitcase, and an orange steamer trunk I never saw him open. I imagined it held his paintings and supplies. A thick yellow light creeping in through the hole was my cue to look through. The old white man had a companion, a small brown and white basset hound with ears that dragged to the floor. While the man painted, the dog lay still as if the man was painting portraits of a sleeping dog.

The white man was our quietest neighbor yet, invisible compared to a roomful of young women or a wife beater. He only spoke to his dog. "Here, Mischa," he'd call in a high pitch.

He hadn't been living there two weeks when he took ill. I suspected something was wrong when the light didn't go on for three consecutive nights. The man was bedridden, day and night, the dog at his side. Yet I couldn't tell anyone without revealing my secret. I prayed that the man got better on his own, or that he at least got well enough to call for help. Like all previous tenants the man had no telephone. Not even mail service. Even we had to rent a post office box. I wandered outside to the back, behind the apartments, my body heavy with guilt. I sat on the wooden bench near the palo verde tree, beneath an infestation of cicadas. I was punishing myself with the constant buzzing and the droplets of fluid my cousins said was cicada piss that could cause boils. My cousins ran in and out of the apartment, slamming the door shut each time. The hollering that followed were my aunts complaining about the noise. I was struck by my ability to own a secret in a place where personal letters were read by more than one pair of eyes, and where whispering into an ear was like whispering into every ear. But I felt no satisfaction.

Only my mother detected something was wrong when she peeked out the door and saw me sitting there, my face as tense as a sock dried to a crisp on the line. She came out to sit next to me and to run her fingers through my hair.

"What are you thinking, you?" she asked.

I blushed. In that overpopulated apartment we rarely had a chance for intimate moments like that one. Any time she showed the slightest affection toward me in front of my cousins, I had to deal with it later in the ravine.

"What a good little boy he is," one cousin would taunt to get the ball rolling.

"He's made of gold," another said, delicately rubbing my sleeve with his index and thumb.

"He's the favorite," my brother added. He joined in most of the time. If not, he too became fair game.

Overwhelmed by too many thoughts, and confused about how to react, I covered my face with my hands and gently nudged my mother with my shoulder.

"What was that?" she asked, letting go of my hair.

I remained silent, sweating behind my hands. I remembered the time I overheard my parents talking about moving out. They had been calculating expenses and figuring budgets on the porch. I didn't realize they were only fantasizing and I jumped to conclusions. I was so happy we were going to have our own place that I immediately went to the room and started labeling our belongings with masking tape and a black marker. When my mother walked in on me I stuttered with embarrassment, trying to explain that I was just pretending, fantasizing the way she and my father had done so on the porch, beneath the warm sun, in the odd privacy of the open air. We had invaded each other, my mother and me, and every awkward moment between us took me back to that day. I sensed I had taken her there as well, which is why she withdrew rather quickly.

"Well, when you're ready to talk to me let me know."

I spread open my fingers and watched her disappear into the apartment. Now I really felt like a fool. A man's life was at stake and I gave up the chance to say something. But how could I reveal to my mother that I had been spying on the neighbors? I was a good boy, unlike my cousins, who got expelled from school, who threw each other down on the floor and used their weight to make each other fart. I showered every evening, I completed my homework, and I was learning English so well I was awarded certificates of merit.

I was the good boy. I vowed never to look through my peephole again. I walked into the house so full of conviction, so absolved, that the first thing I was going to do was plug the hole myself.

That night I finally found a chance to sneak in and do the job with some plaster my grandfather kept handy for all the wears and tears on the walls. We all had to learn to mix and fix because at one time or another we all punched holes, and my grandfather was fed up with making the repairs himself. As a symbolic good-bye to my voyeurism, I decided to take one last look. I lost my breath and a heartbeat when I saw my aunt cooking on the small stove next door. I had to focus repeatedly to make sure I was indeed seeing my aunt moving about in the neighbor's unit wearing her orange plastic apron from the packinghouse. She spoke to the old man in Spanish and he responded in English. The conversation made no sense because my aunt didn't know English and the old man obviously didn't understand Spanish. Yet they managed.

"Aquí está su sopita, ¿eh?"

"I'd like my tea, please."

"¿Y para tomar? ¿Un cafecito?"

"Would you heat up some water, please?"

"¿Agüita? Bueno, pues si ya no se le ofrece nada, pues hasta mañana, ¿eh? Que se sienta mejor."

"Gracias," the old man said, waving his limp arm from the bed, the dog curled up beside him.

There was no way of asking questions without giving myself away. My eye simply followed my aunt into the apartment next door for the next few days. She did some light cleaning, she cooked, and then she disappeared. The dog even took a liking to her, trailing her with its tail wagging. My aunt finally petted it one day and dared to cradle it in her arms like a doll. "Chiquita, Chiquita," my aunt baby-talked. The old man chuckled. So did my aunt.

The man became weaker. I heard my aunt mentioning this to my mother in the kitchen. When they saw me near they started whispering. More secrets. From what little I had heard, I discovered that the landlord had made this arrangement with my aunt as a favor to the old man's son.

That afternoon I saw my aunt sit on the man's bed to spoon-feed him. She displayed a tenderness I had not seen from her before, certainly not on this side of the wall. Here she argued with my grandfather and chased her sons out of the house by throwing things at them. When she was on a rampage she took no prisoners—anyone within range was a potential victim. If she caught someone doing mischief, like that time my cousin played tic-tac-toe on the table with a fork, there was always an accomplice about. *Poros de toro,* my grandmother called the flared nostrils that came with my aunt's uncontrollable rage.

"Which one of you did this with him?" she demanded to the crowded living room of frightened eyes. None of us wanted to tattle.

She took out a belt. "Then I'm going to beat it out of all of you!" And we all dispersed in panic. The last kids out of the room were the first to get it with the belt. My father once joked to my mother that

64

his sister thought she was born with a pair of balls. She had a quick temper, and despite her visits next door she didn't change much.

"I don't like this kind of rice," one of her youngest sons once complained at the dinner table.

My aunt slapped him on the back of the head. "Eat your food, cabrón! What do you think this is, a restaurant?"

My aunt's visits next door ceased as mysteriously as they had begun. The old man either died or was taken away to a more suitable place for his delicate condition. On a sunny afternoon after school my cousins and I gathered to watch a young white couple empty the unit of the steamer trunk and paintings. They offered to give us kids the bed but we all said we didn't want it, though we all slept on the floor. We watched, perched on our bikes, moving back and forth as the couple pulled out canvas after canvas of tree paintings. Those trees were nothing like the ones in the desert.

"What is that?" my oldest cousin dared to ask in his thick accent.

The white guy paused, held the painting upright for us to see and said, "Virginia." That meant nothing to us.

The couple loaded everything into a truck except for the dog and drove off. Since we didn't have any pets we begged to keep it but my grandfather said no. It was too small to be a guard dog and it was a bitch.

"Next thing you know we got a pack of mutts to feed," my grandfather said.

We took turns feeding the dog anyway since it refused to leave its familiar surroundings. My aunt gathered scraps and bones after every meal, though she never went outside herself to cradle it in her arms or to call it "Chiquita." Eventually we got tired of looking after it, especially because it howled all night and kept us awake. We took turns going outside to scare it away. The dog, neglected and malnourished, about-faced one day and scurried off, never to be seen again.

The apartment next door remained vacant for a long time. I had given up the task of sealing the hole with plaster since there was no incentive to look through it anymore, except when the landlords went in to show it to prospective tenants. The unit empty, it echoed with the footfalls of an intruder, which was my cue to run and see who had entered. Once more my heart skipped a beat to see my aunt. She had kept the key to the unit next door from the times she took care of the old man. She simply walked in and stood perfectly still, absorbing the silence of the room and breathing in gently, with concentration. I tried to match her breathing rhythm. Then suddenly her head jerked down and her eye landed point-blank on mine. I held my breath. I even tried not to blink but that was useless; I quickly lost the duel. She held her stance, however, and didn't speak or move. Neither did I. I felt both our bodies relax. It was as if we had agreed to share a secret, a private moment—the hard-to-come-by appreciation of a space burdened by neither touch nor sound.

Thermal, 1981–82
(Our Little Home on Top
of the Garage)

In the family legends, there is one that has always been used to explain the poverty of los Carrillo, my paternal grandmother's branch of the family tree. When this story is told a date is never given but if I start mapping out the generations, this tale involves my grandmother's great-uncle, my great-great-great uncle, who is simply referred to as tío Demetrio. And his famous exchange with el Diablo, Satan himself, most likely took place in the early twentieth century, perhaps in the midst of the Mexican Revolution, somewhere in the untamed mountains near Nahuatzen, Michoacán, where my grandmother's family continues to maintain its roots.

As the story goes, tío Demetrio was tired of the family's lot in life. They were Purépecha Indians living high up in the rough terrains. The men worked the cornfields and kept a modest-sized livestock that supplied the meat, the dairy, and the bartering power in the plazas of the nearby towns. By this time, even the Purépecha had not escaped the influence of Catholicism. Because of their inaccessibility and their metal weapons, they had avoided the conquest of the Aztecs many centuries before, but the Catholics were more subtle invaders, coaxing their way into the hard-to-reach communities, into the humble homes of the Purépecha, and eventually into their hearts and souls, never to leave again.

The Purépecha took to the new religion just as they had taken to the language, Spanish, which was the language of commerce, of access to the modern towns beginning to thrive in the valleys. Catholicism was just another way to survive and move through the streets of the mestizos, all of them Católicos.

For tío Demetrio, Catholicism opened another door, a darker one that hid in the shadows like the swinging doors to the cantina or the cantina's backdoor to the brothel. This one was the door to hell. The church spoke about el Diablo as much as it spoke about Dios. They seemed to be forces to be reckoned with, one just as powerful as the other. And since prayer was doing very little to lift los Carrillo out of an impoverished condition, tío Demetrio decided to attempt another tactic. He would make a deal with el Diablo.

Midnight at the crossroads: tío Demetrio invokes el Diablo's name, offering his fluids as proof of the seriousness of his hailing. He bleeds on himself, urinates and defecates, spits and vomits on himself—desecrating his baptized body before the heavens. After this show of betrayal, tío Demetrio waits and sure enough he has summoned the evil spirits. A dwarfed goat-like creature appears.

Slightly impressed, the creature presents tío Demetrio with a further challenge. He must wait at the crossroads a second and a third night, meeting his visitors face to face, each one more terrifying than the next, as a type of endurance test that will prove he is indeed ready to hold counsel with el Diablo, who may or may not entertain requests. If tío Demetrio fails to stand his ground, however, his punishment for wasting hell's time will be that his family will be cursed with financial hardships and bad luck for the next five generations.

"Are you game?" asks the creature, his grin exposing a sharp set of teeth, like a crocodile's.

Tío Demetrio understands the risks of this wager, but he doesn't imagine himself losing. He has witnessed many horrors in his life—the death of a childhood friend trampled beneath the hooves of a horse, the agony of childbirth, a burst appendix, untreated ulcers and diabetes, alcohol poisoning, snake bites, and the shattering of bone that breaks through the skin. He also knows hunger. In what new ways can fear and uncertainty manifest itself to him? What do he or any of his progeny stand to lose? Tío Demetrio accepts the challenge.

Never underestimate el Diablo. At this point in the story the details become fuzzy, perhaps because not even the wildest of imaginations can envision the creatures that el Diablo sent scampering to the crossroads to meet tío Demetrio. At any rate, even before the first dreaded creature arrived at a complete stop, tío Demetrio's nerves succumbed to his fear, and he fled, forfeiting the challenge and damning the next five generations of his descendants to the ill luck and hardship of the poorhouse.

After my grandmother told me that story she warned me not to repeat it to anybody—especially my grandfather. In fact, when she told it I heard it in snippets since my grandmother immediately ceased talking when my grandfather entered the room. Once she was sewing and speaking at the same time and when he entered she slipped easily into the silence of her task as if she had been quietly pulling on the needle the entire time. And I helped in the farce, pretending I had been quietly observing, not listening. And when she handed me the final piece to the chilling story, I wove it together and saved it in my thoughts to roll around in my head at night as the key to the string of misfortunes that would soon follow. But with these challenges also came hope, because all that time I knew that my cousins and I were the fifth generation, and that this terrible fate would end with us.

On my paternal grandfather's branch of the family tree, there were also stories and legends, but I didn't know many since my grandfather dismissed them as superstitious dribble and a waste of the imagination. He didn't like to dwell in the past so he never spoke about his ancestors or even about his current living relatives. I would find out simple information with time, as I eavesdropped on dinner conversations. It was as if he had deliberately isolated our family from everyone else. Yet I felt our immediate family didn't know how to be alone or how to survive independently of each other.

Whenever a serious matter arose the grown-ups—grandparents, parents, and uncles—congregated in the privacy of a room. And sometimes, quite comically, they all retreated into the bathroom. As a child I watched jealously when these meetings took place. I knew important decisions were being made that would affect us all. I respected the sanctity of these covert meetings until one of my older cousins revealed to me the secret of the assemblies.

"There they go again," he said as the adults converged in the bathroom. "Off to do their witchery."

The word confounded me. "Witchery?" I asked, naively.

"Don't you know, you idiot?" he said. "They go in there to consult the spirits."

"The spirits?" I asked, positive at this point that I was being tricked into another of my cousin's hoaxes.

My cousin leaned in and whispered the big secret in my ear. I refused to believe it.

"You're making this up," I said, so confident in my skepticism that I started to walk away from him.

"If you don't believe me," he said, "look in that cubbyhole above the bathroom closet. You'll see."

Of course, my curiosity won over. No sooner had the grown-ups vacated the bathroom than I scurried in, locking the door behind me. I couldn't imagine how they all fit inside the long, narrow room at once, unless a few of them sat inside the bathtub. I stood on the edge of the basin but I could barely reach the cubbyhole door. I pried it open with my fingertips. It was too dark to see inside. I suspected then that my cousin was probably waiting outside to laugh at me for believing such a ridiculous lie. But I had to prove to myself it was a falsehood so I kept stretching and shoving my fingers into the corner of the cubbyhole to feel around. And then I locked my fingers on it. I tugged at the corner to slide it out. I didn't need to see the whole thing to recognize it for what it was but I needed to see enough of it. Slowly I coaxed it out a few inches into the open. I was looking up at the plain, unadorned backing. To get a good look at the face, I decided to tip it into view, and when I did, the turquoise-colored pointer of the Ouija board scuttled out like a frightened creature and plummeted to the floor.

Because it was plastic, the pointer didn't break. It was shaped like a teardrop with a see-through ring at the narrower end, where individual letters came into focus as it circulated on the board, guided by the faith of hands. I still refused to believe that this was the desperate last resort for the adults in our family. Some people went to church and prayed to the saints and to God; my family entrusted this parlor game. But unlike my cousin, I vowed not to be careless with this information. There was no need for more of us children to see through the illusion of reason and wisdom that seemed to fuel those hush-hush conferences and that produced informed conclusions.

In response to a disconcerting succession of bad seasons, my father and uncle decided to branch out into other working venues, such as construction and demolition. The women always had a place in the packinghouses—warehouses that exclusively hired females to stand behind the conveyor belts to sort fruits and vegetables all day and sometimes well into the evening. They sorted everything from carrots and corn to citrus and palm tree date, smuggling a few samples out in their lunch bags or in the pockets of their plastic work aprons for us kids to enjoy. The healthy goods from the warehouses never looked anything like the wimpy merchandise at the local supermarkets, which always made us wonder where the better crops went. "To Beverly Hills," my grandfather quipped. "Russia," he added.

The men, on the other hand, found jobs with the famous Buxton Ranches. The family saw the good times coming. Everyone in the Coachella Valley recognized the big rancher's contractor and developer logo with the lush purple grapes glaring out from the shipping truck doors. The white trucks themselves were an awesome sight, invading the road like glaciers. My father learned to drive a Caterpillar track dozer, my uncle the tractor, and together with a small team of men they cleaned and leveled the rocky terrain alongside the desert hills to expand the grape fields. My father would come home many afternoons to tell us about the huge machines that plowed through the earth like scooping up ice cream. He would also speak highly of his generous boss, the only white man to ever enter the dinner conversation regularly.

"Mr. Buxton this, Mr. Buxton that," my grandfather once mocked my father. "Can Mr. Buxton guarantee you a job next month, you?"

My grandfather's words contaminated the air like a jinx. Just as quickly as my family saw our luck changing for the better, it took a nosedive for the worse. Within months of each other, two critical events occurred: the packinghouse workers went on strike; and Buxton Ranches went bankrupt. Everyone was forced to look back to the inconsistent hours and low wages of the fields. But since the strikes had caused an industry-wide hiring freeze, everyone was left unemployed and empty-handed.

During that particularly lean holiday season, my eight cousins, my brother, and I all reluctantly accepted that, once again, we wouldn't get anything besides a traditional tamalada and a cup of warm atole. The tamales were delicious, but we consumed them disdainfully, knowing that the celebration of the night was incomplete without presents.

"Now I understand that joke," my cousin said.

"What joke?" another cousin responded.

"Why do Mexicans make tamales for Christmas?"

We all stared at him, waiting for the punch line.

"So they have something to unwrap."

But then, my grandmother came through with an honorable gesture, bringing each of us a humble bag of candy. We took our aguinaldos and sat glumly about the living room, watching our grandfather play records of the music of his generation. At any moment we were expecting him to pull out his accordion, which none of us grandchildren really appreciated though we all admitted he played it well, when suddenly, one of my cousins realized that what we held in our hands was not simply a bag of candies. Hidden inside and showing through the plastic was the stoic face of Abraham Lincoln. We looked over at our grandmother. She placed one index finger over her lips to signify that she had done this without consulting our grandfather, who was a skinflint regardless of the household economy. We therefore proceeded to discreetly exit the noisy living room, the tipsy adults shouting a conversation above the flimsy too-much-bass speakers. In the privacy of the back room we dug into the bags of candy, madly searching for the five-dollar bills. What we found touched us, as an emblem of our grandmother's sacrifice, but also disheartened us by throwing us back into the grim reality of our financial situation. Of course our grandmother couldn't afford to stuff a five-dollar bill into ten bags of candy, so she economized, using five Lincoln bills: she had clipped them in half and allotted one piece per bag. We spent the next five minutes putting the bills back together, uneasy about having been forced to compromise with shared money.

Having no playthings in the house had its benefits. We learned to employ our imaginations, becoming resourceful on the back porch, which overlooked a wild desert landscape: in the palo verde tree we saw a jungle gym, in the mesquite brush, camouflage for hide-and-seek, and in the fine sand, an abundance of a key ingredient in mud play. The noisy cicadas scolded our persistent presence on the back porch during the hottest afternoons of the molting season. Luckily, since there were ten of us children running around causing chaos, we were thrown out of the house to entertain ourselves, away from television. We argued, we reconciled, but always we interacted, never feeling lonely or alone. One of our favorite weekend pastimes was to break into the school for kids with Down syndrome across the street. We pulled out the tricycles and held races all afternoon until we were called in for dinner. Then we took the tricycles back, undamaged for next week's venture.

As our family's finances worsened, the moment neared to make critical decisions about our future. Clearly, this extended family experiment—what we had in México—had been a failure here in the United States as well. After a year and a half, no one had saved money and tensions were high, manifesting themselves in abusive encounters between adults, between children, and between adults and children. My grandfather, who acted the role of the patriarch with relentless authority, was the main culprit. He had been beating my grandmother, had been beating the grandchildren, and had been threatening to beat his daughters-in-law as well. Much of his anger had to do with the relief paychecks my mother and my aunt had been guarding jealously. My grandfather wanted to control the finances exclusively, and he wanted everyone to hand over the funds to him. After my mother returned from the post office one afternoon, he made his demands clearly known. My mother clutched her fists to her chest, tightly clasping the envelope, and refused to comply.

"This money is ours," she said, her voice betraying a confidence I had never heard before.

My mother was beside herself when her father-in-law raised a menacing hand to her. Since I had been a witness to this exchange, my mother made me promise not to tell my father. Later that day, my grandfather singled me out among the group of his grandchildren playing soccer in the schoolyard across the street. I walked out of the game at his command, and followed him to the back of the house, where he thrust a hoe into my hand and demanded that I start to weed. I was surprised because not only had I never maneuvered a hoe but the backyard of the apartment was essentially a desert growing only wild crabgrass and dandelions in such sparse proportions that it had never merited a cleaning before. In fact, the land was so bare we could chase dust devils with our eyes closed without tripping on anything. Slightly apprehensive, I took the hoe into my clumsy grip and began to push the blade into the salty topsoil. Quickly dissatisfied with my performance, my grandfather grabbed the hoe away from me and beat me repeatedly with the metal end. Each time the blade made contact I felt I was being branded with a hot poker.

At the moment of the beating, all the other beatings came back to haunt me, as if the pain were stimulating memory. Making too much noise while your grandfather napped warranted a threesome of welts across your back. Accidentally shattering a plate earned you a knock against the ear that left you too dizzy to locate the pieces on the floor before his anger flared up again and you got a second dose. And thank the long-sleeved discounted shirts from the second-hand stores, or else you wouldn't be able to hide the bruises on your arms from that time you leaned on your grandfather's truck and left your body print on the hood. But how you cursed your luck that the next day was St. Patty's, and that your long-sleeved shirt from the Goodwill Thrift Store didn't possess a stitch of green, and that cruel kids came over to pinch your flesh, unwittingly layering the hurt on your wounds.

My awkward gait that afternoon alerted my mother, who demanded I show her my bruised legs and thighs. Later that night she made me show my wounds to my father, who was forced to acknowledge the escalating violence in that household. The three of us were in the bathroom, where the washing machine was kept. A load of laundry was swiveling inside the tub, and it drowned out my mother's weeping as she struggled with the pant leg of my brother's inside-out pair of jeans.

Our extended family household split apart soon after that, each family going its own way to try to make it alone. A gloomy silence descended upon the house as each family unit packed its belongings in preparation for the exit out the front door. Even the younger children sobbed at the sight of the cardboard boxes collecting in the corners of the apartment. My older cousins and I had been sent on the mission of dumpster diving for moving materials and we took the task seriously, coming home only after we had gathered loads that made us pause for breath every few blocks.

"Are we not going to see each other ever again?" I asked, immediately embarrassed by the sentimentality of my question.

"Don't be stupid," one of my cousins replied. The rest of us realized his response had been impulsive since he didn't elaborate. Instead, as we were nearing the front porch and were received by my grandfather snickering behind his can of beer, my cousin added, "At least we don't have to see him ever again."

Indeed that was the only identifiable blessing for me. My grandfather had fought against the idea of people escaping his grip. My family was the first to leave. When the last box containing what little we owned was squeezed into the borrowed truck, my mother ushered us into the seat and slammed the door once she climbed in. My grandfather had forbidden anyone else from helping us load our belongings and my mother resented the other grown-ups for obeying. I found out later that he had also forbidden anyone from standing outside or even looking out the windows to see us off. When we drove away, the porch was empty as if we were fleeing an abandoned building. Only when the truck reached the street did my grandfather run out onto the porch in a dramatic display of weak triumph to shout at us, "You're going to fail! You're going to fail! You'll be back! You'll be back soon enough!" From the side view mirror I saw my grandfather's image grow smaller and smaller, a tyrant disappearing into his shrinking kingdom.

My family moved into a trailer park in the middle of the desert, but we stayed there very briefly because my mother didn't like the communal toilets or the outdoor showers, where the boys pressed their faces against the stalls to catch a glimpse of the nude women through the cracks in the wood slats.

Our next move was to a small unit on top of a garage located on the same street as my school. It was just the four of us: father, mother, and their two sons. The garage was not an ideal living arrangement either because every morning, when the landlord revved up his truck's engine, the noise would awaken us to the odor of exhaust and motor oil. But this was our home, and it was the only time I remember living as a nuclear family in a decent building—one with its own toilet and shower that we wouldn't have to share with a dozen other people—in the United States. I was so moved by the novelty of the feeling that I felt our new life needed to be documented somehow, so I bought a green pocket diary at the indoor swap meet. Though I eventually lost interest in recording the everyday happenings in our new home, the first entry was inspired by what I knew would be the beginning of a better life. That year I turned eleven. We celebrated our birthdays with a cake and presents. We celebrated Christmas like the people in the United States and didn't celebrate Three Kings' Day like the Mexicans in México. We could afford a weekly Sunday outing to McDonald's to chow on burgers, and best of all we took our first American-style family trip, to Disneyland. All this was thanks to my father's new job as a construction worker, and to my mother's decision to work in the fields, picking grapes beneath the scorching sun, against my father's advice, as he cautioned her about her delicate health and weak heart.

At John Kelley Elementary School, many of us immigrant kids were required to attend speech therapy because of our purported speech impediments. Stuttering, lisping, slurring, and mumbling were but a few reasons teachers gave for our aggravating inability to learn and pronounce proper English. We worked in groups and then held one-on-one sessions with a grown-up. My grown-up was Dolly, a plump southern belle with orange hair. Dolly was old and wore a bright red windbreaker that swished loudly in the hall so that I could always tell she was coming even if my back was turned. She possessed, however, the most beautiful handwriting I had ever seen. Effortlessly, she wrote down her progress notes on unlined paper, her fingers tight around the pencil in a type of graceful dance. In those instances, words became a work of art for me, and letters, the meticulous strokes and malleable lines of a skilled craft. The smallest of words took on magical properties on the page. I knew then that what this woman had to offer was important, and I listened.

Dolly was a talker. Despite my limited English and her drawl, I learned that she came from Texas, that she had a son in community college, that she loved to watch Mike Douglas in his afternoon variety show, and that raisins made her sick. "And isn't that President Reagan a dreamboat?" she declared the day after a State of the Union address. She recited tongue twisters, nursery rhymes, and an impressive list of homonyms that made my head spin. She also introduced me to the infinite number of single-syllable nouns and verbs in the English language, a linguistic characteristic that my native Spanish didn't have. I became fascinated with her Pat-Pet-Pit-Pot-Put. "And yes," she would boast, "every one of those sounds is a word." Under Dolly's tutelage, my fear of English began to dissipate. However, the aversion to the language and school was still strong at home.

In México and in the United States, my homes were without books. My grandparents on both sides were functionally literate, as were my parents and their siblings; none of them had completed an elementary education if they had attended school at all. As a result, my generation didn't appreciate the concept of reading for pleasure or keeping a personal library. The only books around the house were the *TV Guide* and the Bible, and being the non-practicing Catholics that we were, we consulted the *TV Guide* more frequently. The Bible was a gift from the Baptist church we attended the first Sunday of the month because they offered all their attendees a free home-cooked buffet.

Since we were Spanish speakers, schoolbooks with their foreign grammar and diction intimidated and excluded us. We wanted nothing to do with them and we kept them away from the safety of our homes. Our bliss was the television, and also talking over each other at meals in the late afternoons. With time, my older cousins began dropping out of high school to enter the work force; the younger ones began skipping classes, hiding out in the desert brush across the grassy playgrounds. I was learning to enjoy school and had no desire to sneak out in search of more engaging extracurricular activities.

Dolly was shocked to learn that I didn't own a single book. I had imagined that my revelation would earn me a gift, perhaps one of the new picture books with their colorful, glossy covers glaring out from the corner of the classroom. Dolly showed up the following session with a tattered, dull, hardcover book, the spine loose, and its thick innards of pages precariously bound with a yellowed glue.

"Ya like rhymes, don't ya?" she asked.

I nodded my head.

"Poetry," she said. "Read poems aloud every day," she suggested in her Texas drawl. "It'll take care of yer accent."

Hesitantly, I stuffed the huge book into my bag and dragged it home. I was reluctant to open it at first. I found nothing inviting about an old book without pictures, just page after page of words. I recognized the rhymes but not the subject matter. I could read the names, but I had no idea who these poets were: Alfred, Lord Tennyson. Robert Browning. Elizabeth Barrett Browning. William Wordsworth. John Keats. Anonymous.

Weeks later the book remained unexplored. But I wanted to end Dolly's disappointment when, each time we met for speech therapy, she asked, "Are you readin' poetry?" and I responded with an ashamed shaking of my head.

I became a closet reader at first, taking my book with me to the back of the landlord's house or into my parents' room, where I would mouth the syllables softly, creating my own muted music. But as I distanced myself from outdoor games and rough play, I became more comfortable carrying this heavy book to the swings, where I drowned out the screaming and shouting of the other kids to concentrate on the page. The subject matter eluded me but not the rhythms pounding patterns deep in my throat. I found comfort in the book because it was mine and only I could enjoy the secret of its songs since the adults in my home couldn't read English, and my brother wasn't even curious enough to come near it.

Dolly was pleased with me after I told her I was reading my book. She hugged me tightly. The faint smell of coffee and perfume made me take a deep breath so that the moment could linger longer in the memory of her scent.

That afternoon I walked with my class to the bus stop at the far end of the playground. Although I didn't take the bus home, my teacher insisted on dismissing me at the fence with all the other kids. Suddenly Dolly came swishing by and said in my ear, "If you wait a few I have another book for ya."

I became ecstatic. I watched the other schoolkids climb on the buses, and then I watched the yellow busses take off down the road to their respective destinations, and still no Dolly. I became nervous. If I stayed any longer my mother might begin to worry about where I was. If I left then Dolly might get upset at me for not waiting like she had asked. Another fifteen minutes passed before Dolly walked out of a classroom, looking calm in her dark sunglasses until she spotted me.

"Goodness gracious!" she cried out. "I thought ya'd left when I saw the last bus leavin'. I guess I'm takin' ya home."

I saw the panic in her eyes as she rushed over, took me by the arm, and then led me to her car, parked a few yards away. I became so excited to be riding in Dolly's beetle that I couldn't put the words together to explain that I didn't usually take the bus and that I lived within walking distance. The novelty of taking the long route home from school in a car made me give her unclear directions. Repeatedly.

"Oh, no," I said, giggling with embarrassment, "that's not the way either."

Exasperated, Dolly pulled over to the curb, snapped her neck back and yelled, "Well goddammit, kid, don't ya know where the hell ya live?"

I kept a silly grin on my face until I finally steered her to the right place. I stepped out of the car without thanking her or saying good-bye, and watched her small white beetle drive off, vanishing like an ice cube melting. I looked up from the driveway and saw my mother in the kitchen through the high window. She hadn't noticed I had been dropped off by Dolly, my favorite teacher's aide. I recited a few lines of a poem I had memorized to impress Dolly. "The Charge of the Light Brigade." I knew Dolly wouldn't be mad at me the following week when we met for speech therapy. And I wasn't mad at her for forgetting about the book she promised me. I understood Dolly. And Dolly understood me.

I became such an exceptional speller in the fifth grade that my teacher had high hopes I would become a champ. The teacher was Ms. Burnett, an older woman who suffered from a mild case of osteoporosis and had a loose flap of skin hanging down from her chin and neck. The cruel kids in school used to walk behind her and gobble. She was my favorite teacher because we used to correspond through a private journal she made us keep in class. I wrote in mine faithfully once a day.

In this journal I wrote about my family: how I hated seeing my mother's health degenerate; how I hated to see my father drunk; how I had begun to dislike our little home on top of the garage because the toilet would stop working, the refrigerator door was broken, the windows sometimes wouldn't open, and the floor had a few holes in it through which we could see the landlord play on his pool table or climb inside his truck to rev up the engine the way I had seen the racecar drivers do on television. Ms. Burnett wrote back in a calm and composed tone that soothed me. She had a way of making me think through her responses to what I wrote.

Once, for example, I told her a long story about how my father had been looking forward to seeing this war movie on television. My father always watched anything that had to do with the military and the great battles of history. He especially liked movies that dealt with Pearl Harbor or Viet Nam. I would comb through the *TV Guide* each week and keep him informed, and then I'd remind him about it on the day the movie was scheduled to be aired. He never asked us to keep him company and my brother and I rarely did, except when *Hell in the Pacific* was showing because he felt we could learn something from this movie that had no dialogue.

One week I showed him a publicity page in the *TV Guide* for an upcoming movie, and my father immediately became excited by the shot of the desert and the armed men in funny caps standing around in front of camels and a fort. All week he kept asking, *When is it again? At what time?* On the night of the big event my mother made popcorn and her special homemade donuts, and we all sat around in front of the television. The credits started rolling, and there was no music, just the sound of a dry wind and an opening shot of sand dunes glaring out beneath the hot sun.

"This movie's going to be good," my father said, hopeful. He and my mother sat snugly on the couch. My brother and I were lying down on the floor in front of them.

The camera zoomed in on a man looking out at the expansive desert through a pair of binoculars. He began to speak to the man standing behind him in a jeep. They spoke in a language we had never heard before, and then the English subtitles popped up on the screen.

I tried hard to read snippets of the dialogue but I wasn't a fast reader and kept getting stuck on certain words. My father could understand spoken English only. We then tried to follow along guided by the tones of the conversations but the story didn't make much sense. It came across as boring and too talky since an hour into the movie the battle scenes were brief and the bloodshed short on body count. Defeated, we ended up turning the television off and going to bed early.

I wrote to Ms. Burnett that I felt sorry for my father, who had missed out on a movie because there was no way for him to understand it. And I also felt bad I wasn't any help. When we turned the television off, neither of us had said much.

Ms. Burnett responded in her typical manner: one line heavy with wisdom and insight. *You just learned a valuable lesson,* she wrote, *that sometimes words matter plenty, and other times they don't matter at all.*

After a while the other students in class began to notice I had become Ms. Burnett's favorite, but no one resented me for it. I was the shy, quiet kid in the back who had arrived from México a few years before and who turned out to be an accomplished speller. I became the school Spelling Bee champion, beating out the eighth graders as well, with the word "lapidary."

I was a celebrity for a few months and I basked in the attention. Other teachers knew who I was; kids I had never met pointed me out during recess. Ms. Burnett baked me a cake. As John Kelley's spelling champ, I was going on to the next level of competition—the district Spelling Bee. I was given a large packet of vocabulary words to study.

"Maybe your parents can come watch you compete," Ms. Burnett suggested.

I felt my body tingle as I stuffed the packet in my bag. The thought of making my parents part of this project made me uncomfortable. Neither of them would be able to understand what was happening. When we went into restaurants or stores they never spoke up, they simply nodded, smiled, and pantomimed like deaf-mutes. They relied heavily on me to communicate for them. I resolved to spare them any grief by withholding my new endeavor from them.

At home I looked over the list and began to pronounce the words phonetically. I had learned, however, that this was not the way toward every word's proper pronunciation and I needed to memorize both the phonetic and the proper pronunciation in order to visualize the spelling when the word was called out. That was the secret of my success. I couldn't think of anyone to consult about the more unusual words except for Dolly or Ms. Burnett, and both were too busy with their usual teaching duties to go down the list with me. I decided to pose the problem to Ms. Burnett in a journal entry. I also decided to excuse my parents from any sort of participation in the process.

I wrote that besides being a lack of help, my parents did not want me to waste my time on silly lists, and that they believed math and history were more important, so why was I wasting my valuable homework time on preparing for some spelling competition?

Ms. Burnett read my journal entry and believed what I had written. She replied that she intended to do something about it.

I was worried at first, fearing that she was going to pound at my parents' door and demand some sort of justice. But again, Ms. Burnett remained calm and composed.

She found a tutor to work with me before and after school and during lunch. One of the office secretaries made all the meeting place arrangements, and since she was bilingual, she attained my mother's permission in person. My mother was puzzled by the afternoon visit but gave her consent without any objection.

"How odd, you," my mother said after the secretary had left. "What's so wrong with learning words?"

I shrugged my shoulders.

Day after day I memorized words without falling behind in my regular schoolwork. Ms. Burnett had high hopes for me, and she never failed to remind me at the bottom of my journal entries that the competition was so many days away, and that I would win for sure. She always initialed her responses: "PLB." I knew the "P" stood for Peggy because I had seen it in the school yearbook. Through a journal entry I asked her what the "L" stood for, and she responded: "Lurline." I loved that she had shared that information with me.

When the day of the competition finally arrived, Ms. Burnett walked me across the school grounds to the Desert Sands Unified School District office. The conference room was filled with other Spelling Bee champions. At one long table sat the judges and the word caller, all of them dressed in business attire. In the corner stood the newspaper photographer.

The entire episode happened so quickly that the next thing I remember is walking back out of the district office with Ms. Burnett's hand on my shoulder, comforting me. I didn't even place in the competition, but the experience left a lasting impression on me, especially after Ms. Burnett showed me the newspaper column about the event. My name appeared in print. Even my parents were proud when the secretary returned to share the news and paper clipping. To commemorate my achievement they bought me a bookshelf and a bicycle at Zody's. Ms. Burnett and Dolly helped me start my book collection by giving me an order catalog.

It can't get any better, I thought. Until my mother began getting sick.

The first time I noticed something was wrong was when she began locking herself in the bathroom for hours. I could hear her coughing, hacking, and whimpering. My father never seemed to be around during those evenings and for a while I believed his absences were the reason for her illness. Sometimes she'd let the shower run, but this white noise wasn't enough to conceal what I was hearing with my ear pressed against the bathroom door. I thought it impertinent to knock, so I never did. Instead I waited for a sign that she was ready to exit the bathroom so that I could make a dash for the couch on the far wall.

When I wrote to Ms. Burnett about it, her one-line response disappointed me. She wrote that maybe my mother was homesick. I looked up at Ms. Burnett at her desk as I read this. The response was stupid, and she appeared equally as foolish to me in that moment with her old-fashioned glasses perched over her large, pointy nose. She had finally failed me. I didn't understand why she didn't have an answer to my mother's problem. At the moment I wanted to rise from my chair and confront her, yell at her for her useless opinion. All this time I had been writing to her about my mother, about my father, about me. She was supposed to know what I had to do. We had exchanged secrets. She had revealed to me her middle name; I had let her see a letter of endearment I had written for my mother on Mother's Day. She had helped me staple it to a pink construction paper folder and then she had tied a small, white bow on the cover where I had drawn a flower. And what of the time I had shown her the National Geographic article about the kangaroos and how the tiny hairless newborns travel from the womb to the pouch all on their own, vulnerable and pink in their exposed flesh? She had marveled at the photographs and I had blushed with appreciation.

That afternoon my mother was locked inside the bathroom again, but I refused to stay indoors this time to hear her pain, so I rushed down the steps and hopped on my bike, speeding off. I rode down the longest street and then back again. I retraced my path, feeling my face get hot. I tried to steer with no hands, and then with my eyes closed, keeping track of how long I could last before I opened them again.

One-Mississippi. Two-Mississippi. Three-Mississippi. M, I. Crooked letter, crooked letter, I. Crooked letter, crooked letter, I. Humpback, humpback, I.

I wanted to ride right off the road, to the end of the sidewalk, like in my favorite Shel Silverstein book, a gift from Ms. Burnett. I thought I could manage it if I followed the path around the school. I circled again. By the third time I went around, my body aching with exhaustion, my lips trembling because I was on the verge of tears, I zoomed at full speed into the path of a small white Rabbit backing out of the faculty parking lot. I back-peddled to break, skidding as I did so. By then the driver had turned the car around and had shifted into gear, heading right for me. And just when I thought I'd be crushed beneath the wheels, the car stopped, jerking forward at the force of the breaks.

Out of breath, I could feel my heart pounding like a constant kick against my chest. My left hand was slightly skinned and bleeding from the loose crumbs of gravel on the street. Behind the wheel, Ms. Burnett sat frozen with her eyes shut, her mouth open in shock. She clasped the steering wheel and dropped her head on her hands. She couldn't see me mouth that I was sorry. I had lost my voice that instant. So I picked up my bike and quickly rode off, faster and faster until I was so far away I knew I could forget the way back to the last place I would ever face her.

The guitar hanging from a nail on the wall of our little home on top of the garage held a prominent place in my father's memory and heart. This instrument was a symbol of more than music. The dark glistening wood took us back to the homeland, and to Paracho, the nearby town that boasts the finest guitars in the Americas. The thin pick trapped behind the strings was a remnant of the fireside gatherings at dusk, at which I used to keep my hands close to the flame, my mouth busy with a piece of tortilla toasted over the glow of kindling. My father once told me that eating a burnt tortilla kept the witches from sucking my blood, so I used to crunch loudly enough for the witches to hear.

On those wintry nights my father usually played the guitar because he owned the largest repertoire thanks to his days with Dinastía. That's another memory pinned to the south wall—a portrait of five attractive young men dressed in pink slacks and vests (my father the second one from the right in narrow-frame sixties sunglasses) and all sporting identical patent leather shoes. Dinastía.

My father believes that women love musicians. To aspire to be in a musical group is to aspire to be a lover. And the guitar is a lover's choice weapon. A love poem turned to song weakens the woman's defenses. Confronted with it, she easily gives up a smile, a laugh, perhaps a bat of the eyelash. All the while, the man caresses the guitar, flirtatiously holding it close to his body in a show of passion. The guitar's sensuous curves and its smooth back are, after all, a suggestion of the female body. To play the guitar is to practice lovemaking; to master it is to prove one's skills in the art of carnal pleasure.

I imagined my father using his talent to court and serenade my mother the way men did in those romantic black-and-white Mexican films from the fifties. At the completion of a ballad, the beautiful señorita consents to bless the handsome singer by throwing him a kiss over the balcony as a portent of more fiery things to come. Hence another valuable lesson: learn to play an instrument, learn to sing, get the girl in the end.

But even in my prepubescent age—already familiar with the politics of courtship, having seen the singer-señorita exchange on television and having heard the Mexican love songs on the radio, both to the point of exhaustion—I had no desire to become a Don Juan. In fact I didn't want to please a woman. I only wanted to please one man — my father.

Effeminate and demure, I always became self-consciously boyish around my father. When I hurt myself I tried to cuss like a male instead of simply yelling out *Ay!* like a girl. I played more aggressively with my brother's action figures and avoided having them sit around at a pretend restaurant with a building block jukebox that prompted Han Solo to ask Luke Skywalker to dance. At the dinner table I discussed P.E. soccer matches, highlighting the exploits of the better players, keeping to myself the soccer captain's usual decision to make me goalie because I was the slowest runner and worst kicker. I despised sports and the competitive nature of elementary schoolboys. I wasn't the last one picked; I was the one left over.

My father had maintained his muscular physique and a left cauliflower ear from his years as an amateur boxer. He was small in stature, but his booming voice made him grow in size. Like a speaker behind a podium, when he said something he grabbed everyone's attention. And his tolerance to pain was impressive. Once my brother slammed the car door on my father's hand. Despite the swollen purple fingers, my father's eyes didn't water, though mine did. On another occasion he called us in to watch him pluck the entirety of a toenail that had been damaged after he had stubbed his toe. He didn't flinch like we had.

When my younger brother and I outgrew our desire to simply listen to the guitar, my father had been more than eager to teach us. A traditional Mexican ballad was one of the heartfelt ties to México. I wanted to be as sentimental as my father, lifting my chin up at the final envoy as if the song had been sent off on an uncertain yet hopeful journey. Most of all I wanted to impress him with his own ring finger-thumb trick: using those two fingers he'd switch off plucking away at the strings, his hand shaking excitedly at the speed.

At the first lesson we encountered a setback.

Because I was left-handed I was deemed clumsy and awkward, especially after the infamous fly-swatting incident back in the old apartment. My grandfather had asked me to kill the flies buzzing around in the kitchen. I took the swatter with my left hand. And because of a nearsightedness that was not to be diagnosed until many years later, I missed each time. Furious, my grandfather commanded: "Use your right hand, you!" The pressure made my aim worsen. SWAT! SWAT! No luck.

"Your right hand!" my grandfather repeated.

Those words haunted me for years because my cousins, witnesses to my ineptitude, repeated them whenever I threw a weak ball or accidentally dropped a spoon. "Your right hand!" they'd scream. Then they'd limp their wrists for added humiliation.

My father became disheartened when I held the guitar with the neck pointing to the right, my left fingers anxious to strum.

"You're holding it the wrong way," he said, correcting the direction of the strings immediately by flipping the neck to the left. "Like this."

The weight felt bulky against my left shoulder. My right hand, that bumbling hand that couldn't kill flies, was now burdened with the responsibility of rhythm. My fingertips scratched; they didn't graze the strings. I poked, I didn't press down. The instrument wailed and screeched in my arms like a wounded cat. In contrast, my brother cradled the guitar with a gentleness that produced delicate sounds. Each of his beginner's notes soared in harmonious flight. Our mother listened patiently from the kitchen. In the back of my mind I secretly wanted to stand next to her behind the stove, frying those delicious homemade donuts on the skillet. Her nails glistened with a coating of butter, grease, and sugar. When she took her thumb into her mouth to lick it, my mouth watered. Later that night I too sucked my fingers after handling a donut, but it didn't taste quite as clean and sweet with that lingering metallic flavor of guitar strings.

After a few weeknights of tolerating my wooden touch, my father gave up, but with the assurance that once we got a guitar for left-handers, I could enroll once again in his solo teacher music school.

At the look of disappointment in my eyes he quickly added, "But why don't you learn the songs. That way you can accompany your brother's playing."

That's when we came across a second setback.

I was never a bad singer. In fact I was quite good. In school I had joined the chorus, though my mother had asked me not to reveal this to my father. When we still lived in Michoacán, my mother's family had even considered sending me to audition for Los Niños Cantores de Morelia, just a few towns away. Morelia housed the oldest conservatory in the Americas, and Los Niños Cantores was México's answer to the Vienna Boys Choir. But that pipe dream vanished without an explanation. I deduced—a guess that was later confirmed by my mother's insistence that I keep the school chorus a secret—that my father had a low opinion of boys who sang not like men, but like women.

At six, my high-pitched voice made me a budding contralto. However, a girlish voice was much more endearing on a six-year-old than on an eleven-year-old. According to my cousins I sounded like a maricón, a sissy. I could only imagine what my father thought when I hit those high, shrilly notes.

My brother once went around the house imitating a choir of singing nuns we saw on television. In falsetto he kept crooning, "Dominique-nique-nique" until my father heard him. My father raised his hand and threatened to strike if my brother didn't shut up. My brother jumped and cried out, very much puzzled, "What? What did I do?" No answer.

I knew why, and it shamed me to think I embarrassed my father with that feminine voice. No matter how much I tightened my throat the pitch didn't get lower. Two years younger, my brother's voice was already thick and heavy. The question popped into my head for the umpteenth time: What if I was meant to be a girl? How many afternoons on the way back from school had I been reminded of that possibility when I stumbled across a dandelion puff? I'd pick it up, shut my eyes, blow on it to scatter the tiny parachutes, and then I'd wish I were a carefree, light-hearted, simple girl. Like one of my female cousins, who at nine, had already mapped out a life: "I'm going to get married, have two sons, and be that lady who blows the recess whistle at school."

I wanted to be a girl because I wanted to do girl things: comb my long hair, sit on the back of the pickup truck and whisper secrets, and wash dishes and stick my tongue out at the boys when I caught glimpses of them playing ball through the window over the sink. All the boy activities just seemed like too much work.

To relieve my father of his teaching duty to his left-handed, high-pitched son, I feigned loss of interest in both the guitar and the songs, and instead I watched reruns of *Charlie's Angels* at low volume. In the background I heard my father coaching my brother, "Do, do-re-mi, do-re-mi-fa . . ." as they picked at the strings together.

I still had, however, my school chorus, where my high notes and dedication were better appreciated. I had even secured a spot on the first row for the upcoming Spring Recital, which only meant I had all the songs memorized. Everyone from the second row and back kept the chorus sheets hidden from view behind the person in front. Three afternoons out of the week I was excused from P.E. to attend rehearsals. I was the only boy in the fifth grade willing to make that sacrifice, so I became the only boy left in the chorus.

At about this time my mother fell ill from a recurring heart condition and had to be hospitalized. I held back the tears because my father did, and so did my brother. At night her absence was painfully obvious because none of us came out of the shower smelling like scented talc or body lotion. It was as if the apartment had suddenly gone dull and sterile. My father tried to distract us with card tricks and trips to the drive-in. I got to ride in the front. It felt odd. My mother's seat in the car was too big for me. Yet it also thrilled me. I had been promoted somehow to an adult place, a woman's place.

Coming home from school to an empty apartment allowed me to explore my mother's private things: her bras, her panties, and her makeup kit. I absorbed the smells and textures, releasing the memory of my mother back into the air. But after a while the strength of those smells took over, seizing my senses in a way not even music could. I became mesmerized by the erotic power of it. I wanted to own that power. I imagined the scent wafting over to the school bully, thawing his hard face into a pillow of lovesickness.

Each afternoon while my brother lost himself among the neighborhood streets on his dirt bike, I practiced dabbing rouge on my cheeks in slow and delicate circles just as I had seen my mother apply it to her own soft skin. I pushed her roll-on deodorant against my chest, spotting my T-shirt with strong traces of perfume. I powdered my bare underarms and neck. I would have worn the bra, but I couldn't figure it out, so I simply flung it across the room a few times, quickly rushing over to press my nose into the cups. The panties were too big so I stuck my hand through one of the leg openings and stretched the material over my shoulder. The panties would slip down and I'd pretend my bare shoulder had become exposed. "So sexy," I'd declare.

This daily after-school routine reached yet another peak when I dared to open the nail polish—red as only my mother could wear on a Sunday morning. We weren't a church-going family, so my mother's primping was in preparation for our weekly visit to a fast-food restaurant or to the grocery market.

I twisted the cap off the nail polish, took in the sharp odor, and watched the thick liquid slide down to the tip of the brush, flattening into a drop of blood. I considered my short, stubby nails and wondered about my mother's method: Stroke, shake, blow. Stroke, shake, blow. I imitated her strategy, recognizing that the unevenness of the paint job could only be worked out with practice. I managed to apply one complete coat by the time my father came home unexpectedly. In our little home on top of the garage, opening the front door was like removing every wall at once—there was no place to hide.

There I was, his firstborn, his namesake, experimenting with fingernail polish. I froze up, hoping I'd become invisible. I tried to trigger a seizure but my brain went numb. There was nothing I could do to distract his attention away from the shabby paint job and the spilled polish. The panties crawled down my arm and caught at the elbow. My face burned with fear. All I saw were my father's eyes growing in size and intensity as he took in the whole living room without blinking. Would collapsing at his feet begging for mercy help? It was worth a try.

But to my surprise he suddenly looked away without uttering a word and headed straight to the bathroom. He spent enough time in there for me to clean myself up, though it seemed I had wiped and hidden every last shred of evidence within seconds of his closing the bathroom door. There was an uncomfortable gap of time left over for me to sit on the couch and do nothing but contemplate the bodily harm that would be inflicted on me. I even thought of injuring myself first to diffuse my father's fury and to spare myself the anxiety of the wait for punishment. The smell of nail polish remover lingered in the air. I picked at the cotton hairs caught on my chewed nails. Then, without giving it much thought, I unhooked the guitar and pressed it tightly against me like a shield. Sliding my hand across the smooth surface consoled me. Biting into the triangular plastic pick kept my teeth from chattering. My jagged nail digging into the ridges of the strings produced the only sound in that dead silence.

When my father finally exited from the bathroom, it was as if he had forgotten what he had just seen. The bathroom door slid open, my breath stopped, and instead of lunging straight into me like the bull to the matador, my father quietly stepped into the kitchen and began to cook our dinner. I resisted the urge to follow him with my eyes. Instead I strummed absent-mindedly on the guitar as I concentrated on the clattering of pots and pans. With the frying of the oil and garlic, I pretended that it was my mother behind the stove, and that soon she'd ask me to stop playing with that guitar and search for the good tomatoes in the fridge.

I replayed the entire scenario in my head repeatedly, imagining a different outcome if it had been my mother who had opened the front door.

"Tonto," she would have said, perhaps amused. "Put that away before your father sees you."

She might have even removed the nail polish herself, wiping off the redness with a firm but delicate hold on my hands.

My mother corrected my habits and mannerisms repeatedly. She kept warning me about that limp-wrist swat on the shoulder I sometimes gave my brother when he was pestering me; she had asked me not to imitate the school drill team exercises in the living room; she told me to stop putting my fists on my hips when I was lost in thought; and she absolutely refused to let me play with dolls.

Besides my brother's *Star Wars* action figures I never actually kept dolls in the house, but I had this little game in which I tied a knot at one corner of a bandanna. The knot became the head, the small piece of cloth at the top was like a gush of hair and the larger piece of cloth under the knot was like a dress. I created two, sometimes three of these rag dolls and made up little scenarios for them on the couch, which became my stage.

At first my mother didn't seem to care if I acted out these fantasies. My game kept me out of her way as she cooked dinner in the kitchen. I enjoyed staying home in the evenings instead of joining my rambunctious brother in the streets. In fact for the longest time I didn't think anyone had noticed my nightly entertainment until that evening my brother and I got into an argument over the television. I can't recall how it started, but it ended when, as a strategy to shut me up, my brother exposed me to my father.

"He's so stupid," my brother said. My father was drinking a beer at the kitchen table while my mother cooked. "Look at this stupid game he plays." My brother pulled out a bandanna and performed the knot trick. He showed it to my father. "Dolls!" he exclaimed.

A lump in my throat prevented me from quickly defending myself. I was completely humiliated. All I could squeeze out of my throat was: "They aren't dolls. They're snakes."

My brother mocked my explanation. "Snakes?" he said. "Snakes don't go shopping on the couch."

"That's enough, you," my mother said. She lifted the greasy metal hand of the spatula.

"But it's true," my brother persisted. "He makes them talk and say stupid sissy things to each other."

"Stop it, I said." My mother took one step forward. The threat worked and my brother said no more.

Meanwhile, my father looked away as if he had not heard a thing, and that made me feel even worse—I had shamed him. My mother turned toward the stove and looked at me through the corner of her eye. I stood frozen with guilt.

That night while I pretended to sleep in the dark, my mother crouched down to whisper in my ear that I was not to play that game again. And I never did.

I learned quickly that my mother's actions were not necessarily meant to protect me, but to protect my father. My father didn't beat me for being a sissy, but I knew it bothered him greatly, so it became my mother's responsibility to censor and punish me. At her kindest my mother pinched me from behind, like the time I started to comb my cousin's hair on the steps while my father was parking the car. Never mind that my cousin had asked *me* to do her the favor. My mother grabbed the brush away from me, pushed me back, and took over nervously. My mother's reaction didn't make much sense to me at that moment.

For extreme offenses in my father's presence I got the belt. One occasion I remember quite clearly was when I walked out of the shower with a towel wrapped turban-style on my head. I had no idea I was doing anything wrong because I had seen my mother do this every night. I liked the way a few damp strands of hair stuck to the skin of her nape and forehead. I tried to imitate this look right down to the wet body talc and traces of roll-on deodorant at the wrinkles of her bare armpits. My mother would be impressed, I thought, and I kept right on thinking that as I stepped out of the bathroom. My waltz had been carefully choreographed from the bathroom to the living room so that everyone in the house got to see me. But no sooner had I made my way to the kitchen than my mother yanked the large white towel off my head, sending me stumbling to the side. My father caught the second part of this awkward dance from the living room couch. With one swift step out and back into the kitchen my mother held in her hand my father's belt and gave it four solid swings. The leather coming into contact with my fresh-out-of-the-shower skin made a clean snapping sound I couldn't quite connect to the hot stinging on my arms and legs.

I didn't have to get whipped too many times before I realized that being a sissy-boy had no place in our home. And yet I could not stop myself. I had no control over my girlish behavior. It came so naturally. I had crushes on boys, I hung out with my female cousins, and my best friend in school was an even bigger sissy than I was. I tried only once to approach the subject about our girlie selves but I didn't get the response I wanted.

"What do you mean?" Carlos asked me. Everyone called him Carla and he reveled in that. We were swaying on the swings in the playground after school. Since we walked home we didn't leave until we waved good-bye to the last school bus as it hit the road, the boys in the back of the bus yelling out "Adiós, jotos!"

"Well, you know," I said. "We don't like sports and our friends in school are all girls."

"And what's wrong with that? I'd rather hang out with girls than with those nasty boys. I hate boys. Don't you?" He leaned back and let his head drop. His hair was long and curly. My parents would never let my hair grow that long.

"Well, what does your family think about that?" I asked.

He leaned forward and planted his feet on the ground to stop swaying. "My family loves me," he said with conviction. "They don't care how I am."

I confirmed the truth to this statement when I attended his twelfth birthday party later that year. There was Carlos in all his glory with a red construction paper crown on his head that no matter how you looked at it resembled a tiara. Carlos and his mother hugged frequently and giggled like girls. The house was decorated with frilly streamers and balloons that were dipped in glitter. Carlos shrieked each time someone new showed up at the door and shrieked again when he accepted each gift. But what really shocked me was his father's indifference to the whole spectacle. A big man with a heavy growth of beard on his face, Carlos's father simply stepped in and out of the house unfazed. He didn't even flinch when Carlos threw his skinny arms around his neck and shrilled with excitement. Even that was a bit much for me. I blushed on his father's behalf and resolved at that moment that I would stop being Carlos's friend. How dare he get away with all of this? How dare his family love him for it? I was especially angry at his mother, who seemed to encourage her son's outbursts by running to him and working him up about any little thing.

"The cake, Carlos, the cake!" she would say one minute, flapping her arms in the air, and "The games, Carlos, the games!" the next. And every time Carlos let out a high-pitched cheer that annoyed me to the point of disgust.

Later that evening my father came to pick me up from the party. Carlos had tried to convince me to stay for the sleepover but I had had enough of him, and the idea of watching him play Carla well into the night did not appeal to me. When my father's car pulled into the driveway I noticed my mother's absence right away so I quickly asked, "Mami?" My father's silence could only mean one thing: that my mother was sick again.

My mother was getting sick more frequently. Ever since a rheumatic fever at the age of seventeen, my mother had been diagnosed with a weak heart and had been susceptible to bouts of cold sweats and body aches. I would come to associate my mother with hospital sheets, plastic bedpans, and white trays of soft foods that glowed with clear colors under the bright glare of the fluorescent lights. It was ironic how my mother's condition made me invisible. The focus shifted from my behavior to her deteriorating health. But even then I didn't have the energy to be girlish or silly because I had entered a deep state of depression. My mother was everything to me. I was everything to her. My brother acted like my father; I acted like my mother. My brother liked going hunting with my father; I enjoyed watching my mother when she cooked or put on her makeup or when she picked out a matching purse for her special occasion outfits. My brother was my father's boy; I was my mother's. I eventually came to think of myself as my mother's companion. In the absence of my father and brother, indeed the masculine element of the household, my mother and I got along fine. We exchanged fotonovelas (the Mexican picture books of soap operas with only snippets of dialogue) because she understood my love of reading and my interest in keeping myself literate in Spanish. I enjoyed keeping her company in her ESL classes. And though she could barely write, I loved her signature, a lower case script from beginning to end, and with so many *a*s—Avelina Alcalá—the name was pure music.

Even better than our outings to night school were our evenings together at home as we waited up for my father, who was out drinking. He was one of those drunks who came home soaked in sorrow, begging forgiveness for an act he would repeat the following night. As we waited for my father to arrive in tears, my mother would speak softly into a cup of tea cooling off in her hands.

"We'll have to plan a trip to Michoacán soon," she said one night. Her statements usually hovered in the air without direction. And I sat there with her to listen to them. The nights were quiet and the kitchen was small. I could hear my mother gulp down each sip of tea. She had small, light-skinned hands with nails that didn't grow long because she worked in the vegetable packinghouses sorting corn and carrots in the winter, and picking grapes in the summer. Yet I suspected her hands were smooth. I don't remember actually touching them. Even though those hands had hurt me on many occasions I refused to think of them as rough or cruel. On those long nights that I sat beside her, my head nodding off to sleep, I forgave her. I understood that that's just how it was going to be.

"Go to bed, you," she would say to me when she noticed I was falling asleep in my chair. There was no sense of urgency or demand in her voice. It was as if she had to say it out of maternal obligation though she didn't mean it. I was sure she wanted me to stay so I stayed.

As soon as my father arrived the usual drama ensued: the tears, the reprimand, the slow journey into the bedroom, the silence. We could hear his heavy steps coming up the wooden stairs. He'd fumble with the keys for a minute or so before managing the door. When my mother got up to help him inside I walked quietly to the couch, too sleepy to care about anything anymore.

The guitar, in the meantime, was collecting dust because my brother had lost interest in anything at all. He had been caught skipping school a few times and the school principal was concerned about his increasingly violent behavior with other schoolboys. And I, too, was moving forward in my own way: I had developed a crush on another man, another Dinastía member, pictured second from the right in that famous portrait on the south wall of the apartment above the garage. He was the musician with the strong masculine jaw and the funky pair of sunglasses. Both lenses reflected the camera's flash. For months I stared very intensely into those splashes of light, attempting to penetrate through those lenses. I just had to discover—I just had to find out—if indeed he was looking back at me.

Summer's Passage

"Son, are you awake?"

" . . . "

" . . . "

"What do you want?"

"Me? Nothing. I just thought if you were awake we could talk."

"About what?"

"Whatever. Your friends. Do you have many friends in Riverside?"

"A few."

"Any special friends?"

"They're all special."

"And . . . ?"

"And nothing."

"Well, tell me more. Tell me anything. How did you meet them?"

"Which one?"

"Any one of them."

My father and I exchange words in the dark. I can't even tell what time it is, but I know it's too early in the morning to be having this conversation on the bus, especially about my special friends. I can just make out the sky becoming clearer over the horizon and the dominant sound is still the rough engine shifting gears as it speeds onward to Michoacán. And then something takes hold of me. A need for sex, but not just sex with anyone; I'm hungering for my lover.

I want to believe that my lover is sitting up on the edge of his bed at this hour, his face inside his hands, letting the streetlight stripe the interior of the lonely room through the slits of the Venetian blinds. His body is a silhouette, but solid, which makes the expression of his grief more beautiful, like a flower growing out of rock.

I remember the times he rises in the predawn hours and how he sits back on the bed to have a cigarette. When he exhales, the smoke shoots out inside a heavy sigh that tells me he's more than smoking. I'm saddened that I'm not there to respond to him.

It's funny how memory works, where all that is recollected never comes back in its original form. To keep myself from going crazy with lust, I look at the two white marks on my hand.

"Is something wrong, querido?" I asked him on the night he gave me those scars. He took a few more drags from his cigarette, but he didn't answer. I repeated the question, and added, "You can tell me. You can tell me anything."

And he did. As my eyes adjusted to the dark, the stress on his face became more and more visible as I witnessed the filling in of the soft human features into the opaqueness of his head. He told me that when he was a boy his father had raped him.

His father had been out drinking as usual, and his mother locked him out of the house to teach him a lesson, forbidding anyone to let him in. The violent banging against the door woke him up and he opened his bedroom window for a better look. His father was kicking with the foot that still had a shoe; the other foot was bare and the second shoe was nowhere in sight. When he laughed at this comical scene, he alerted his father, who seized on the chance to get inside. His father crawled in through the window and my lover watched uneasily as he removed his clothes and settled into the bed to sleep. He wanted to avoid his mother's wrath at his betrayal, so my lover reached over his father's naked body to grab for a pillow in order to sleep more comfortably on the floor. He imagined how all of these details would entertain the family over breakfast the following day, his mother forgiving all as she stood over the stove, giggling. And that's the thought that took him into peaceful sleep, until the violent pain of penetration woke him in the middle of the night, his screams held in by the vice grip over his jaw.

"I would have thought it was all a bad dream the next day," my lover said, "if it hadn't happened again before he left my room in the morning."

"I don't understand," I say, my voice shaking at the enormity of the revelation. "Did you tell your mother? Did you go to the police?"

My lover calmly stretched out his arm. "Give me your hand," he said.

I offered him my right hand in comfort, but as soon as we made contact he swung his other arm around and burned me with the cigarette. The sting shocked me and I pulled my body in as I squeezed the knuckle of my wounded hand, unable to do anything but cry as I looked at the two spots of white flesh exposed when the cherry skipped on my flesh and burned off skin.

"That's for asking stupid questions," he said. "Now leave me alone before I burn your balls off."

The memory of the sting makes my eyes water. For months afterward I was unable to see a lighted cigarette without rubbing the scar tissue or without feeling warmth glowing underneath the marks. I'm doing precisely that when my father, sitting next to me on the bus, reaches over and places his hand over mine.

"Are you going to tell me a story?" my father asks.

I breathe in deeply and expel the heaviness of my thoughts.

"Let me sleep a little longer," I say. I snuggle into my seat and drift off into uneasy sleep.

When I wake up again it's only the second morning of the trip. I'm relieved that I'm still moving away from Riverside, but the desire for my lover has not subsided. And I can't imagine myself walking into the tiny, stinky bathroom stall to masturbate on a shaky bus, so I squirm in my seat, pressing my fists on my erection. Outside the skies are dark and cloudy. I can tell we're in Nayarit by the lush vegetation and mountains that tower over this state and continue into Jalisco and Michoacán. My body feels numb from another night of restless sleep and I'm grateful to be sitting next to a window that can actually open. But soon the rain starts coming down. I pull out my light jacket from my backpack and use it as a cover. My father must have put his on sometime while I was snoozing. He looks up at the ceiling of the bus. I look up as well and find the leak he's staring at.

"I guess we'll have to swim out of the bus," I say.

"You know how to swim now, you?" he asks. I blush.

On the second or third stop after we cross the Sinaloa-Nayarit border, Zacatecas, my father's other traveling companion, gets off the bus and I'm pleased. I have grown annoyed hearing his voice call out to my father from the back of the bus all this time. In the end he didn't even do that but simply whistled. When people whistle-talk it irks me. It reminds me of my grandfather flagging down my grandmother at the swap meet and of the many other women who also turned around because they mistakenly thought their own husbands were summoning them. Whistling to people is like whistling to dogs.

When Zacatecas bends down to shake my father's hand I glare at him. He's taken aback by this but graciously says good-bye to me as well. I'm further dismayed when he stands at the front of the bus and gives his blessings to the rest of the passengers, wishing them a safe arrival home. People respond kindly and I want to scream out in exasperation.

"He's a good man," my father says. I leave it alone.

The mood becomes dull for the rest of the day without Zacatecas. The bus passes through Nayarit without any delays, but I can't help but gawk at the greenery and at the mango trees with fruits that hang like testicles on the branches. Soon we're in the state of Jalisco. A stretch of mountains in Jalisco appears desert-like because they have been cleared to let the maguey plant flourish. From this plant comes the tequila.

"Is your mouth watering?" I ask my father, who looks at me puzzled. "Nothing, nothing," I say, aware that perhaps this comment went a little too far, even for me.

Also I feel like a hypocrite. My father's drinking has always been the perfect scapegoat for all of our family ills. My mother never forgave him for that, so I kept this grudge alive after her death. The truth is I have also learned about the pleasures of intoxication. But with my lover, drinking is a glamorous evening venture, not the sloppy, word-slurring, mouth-drooling after work activity my father engages in. My father and his beer buddies stand outside in dirty clothing, sipping out of cans in paper bags. When the night catches up to them nobody bothers to turn on a light. The bodies darken and their voices get louder until someone's wife sends a child to call his father home, breaking up the party until the next time. No one will know exactly how much has been consumed until the following morning when the sun shines on the discarded containers scattered on the yard.

My lover and I have cocktails—vodka martinis or manhattans. We attend socials at private clubs or reunions in fancy bars with mood lighting designed to make people look thinner and younger. No one stumbles home—they are escorted to a cab or to someone's car. It never occurs to me that my father could drive while drunk; I have never seen that happen. But my lover does, swerving through the freeways as I push my feet up against the dashboard to keep myself steady. The cassette tape plays music we have just been listening to at the club. I never worry about the danger because he always gets us home safely, me tipsy or nearly passed out in the passenger seat. The only part I don't like about these nights is that my lover gets horny and fucks me dry as soon as he peels my pants off. Even though I am numb with alcohol the sessions are still uncomfortable and painful.

"That's a good bitch. That's a good bitch," my lover spits into my ear, and I clench my teeth, wondering if the women of my family ever had to deal with a man like this. I can't picture my parents in this role, not even when I recall the only time I have heard my parents have sex—my father huffing, my mother whimpering, but both complicit in the strenuous scuffle of passion. After this rough exchange with my lover, he always sits back and smokes a joint. I need another drink.

When I drink I believe I'm drinking much differently than my father. My father's drinking is an embarrassment to the family. My drinking is a way to be a part of my lover's world.

In my lover's world there are also drugs. Crystal meth, cocaine, pot. I like crystal because it keeps me up all night, and I can read an entire book in one sitting, my nose twitching from the flaring nostrils.

"I can't believe you're wasting time on that," my lover chides me. He thinks he's much more productive, mixing tapes until six in the morning for our road trips up to Los Angeles or San Francisco.

I push myself into the seat on the bus. My throat tightens from the memory of snorting crystal. I try to relax my breathing. My father notices this and becomes alarmed.

"Do you need to vomit?" he asks.

I shake my head.

"Do you need water?" he asks. "We'll be making a stop soon."

"Quit it," I tell him. "I just need some air."

My father freezes the look of pity on his face. He always puts this mask on as a last recourse, when he doesn't know what to say or how to react.

I shut my eyes. I want to make my father go away, but I can feel his warm breath, and it's annoying me.

My lower lip trembles as I recall the evening my grandmother told my brother and me over dinner that our father had abandoned us. Less than a year after my mother's death, my father had moved out of the house while we were away at school. He had gone off to marry a woman with three sons of her own. She was carrying his child. As she revealed the last piece of information, I dropped the spoon on the plate and flung myself across the room in a fit of spasms and tears.

What no one knew was what had happened the night before. In the two-bedroom unit, my grandparents occupied one bedroom; my father, brother, and I the other; but I opted to sleep on the living room couch, where I could sneak peeks into the refrigerator at midnight, or watch the television programming of my choice, or simply read with the weak kitchen light in silence. I had been on a strange exercise kick recently, inspired by all the sightings of taut bellies and pubescent pecs at the school gym. I wanted to be with these young bodies. I wanted to be more like them. So I started doing sit-ups and push-ups before going to sleep at night. I did all this with the lights off, as if the blackness could help me push this fantasy for musculature forward. I had just completed a second set of sit-ups when my father walked out in his white underwear that glowed in the dark.

"What are you doing?" he asked. I didn't answer.

Suddenly, he swung around and dropped on top of me, pinning my head down with his forehead, his body balanced on his arms. When he smiled his teeth also radiated their whiteness. My breathing quickened and I was embarrassed to be feeling an erection. He lowered his body closer to mine, and his belly came into contact with my arousal. But I couldn't move. I tried to pry him off me but he wouldn't let me, so I simply succumbed, waiting to find out, wanting to experience what he'd do next. And then, just as unexpectedly, he jumped off and disappeared into the bedroom again, leaving me flushed and confused about what had just happened between us on the living room floor. The next day, he was gone.

Una desbaratada, my grandmother called it, this nervous breakdown that kept me out of junior high school for nearly two months. My grandfather grew tired of shuttling me around from one doctor to the next, and of picking me up from the nurse's office in school, until finally the school counselor suggested a psychologist.

"In all of our family history we've never had a crazy person," my grandfather replied with outrage. But he agreed to it, if only to appease the school counselor.

My grandfather drove me to the psychologist, a tall, neatly primped woman who kept peeling her eyelids back after every other sentence she spoke. Her suggestion, after less than an hour of talking to us, was that I should be thoroughly evaluated at a professional facility. My grandfather didn't even wait to leave the office before he went off on a tirade.

"All this talk is useless," he said. "Can't you just give him some pill or something? What kind of a doctor are you? I'll be damned if I'm going to waste any more time on this kid. If he's that damaged then take him outside and bash his head in with a rock!"

In the psychologist's eyes I saw the strange hurt of empathy as she watched my grandfather drag me out of her office. I spent the next twenty-two days in Mexicali, ensconced in my aunt's house until my grandfather agreed to take me back. My father never once came to see me.

As I look into my father's pitiable face on this bus to Michoacán, I have the urge to confront him about all of this, but I can't. I wish he could read my mind to spare me the energy of having to put it into words, everything from my resentment for his having left me to the fact that I'm gay and that he has nothing to do with that. My body aches from the restraint.

"What's wrong? What is it?" my father keeps asking. I shake my head, holding back tears.

When he notices that other passengers are looking at us, my father releases a nervous laugh. He leans over to press his head against mine. I redden. He used to do this when I was a boy in Zacapu; it was his way of expressing affection.

"Let me see that smile," he says.

I push him away. "Cut it out," I demand. I turn my body around and fold into myself, my kneecaps on the armrest.

His eyes look down.

I skip all meals that day, munching on a bag of candied peanuts I bought during one of the brief stops. But my father keeps bringing me small cartons of juice that I accept without speaking. The emotional seizure has exhausted me, so I sleep soundly for the first time since the journey began. Because more passengers have been leaving than boarding the bus, entire rows of seats become vacant. My father moves to another pair of seats so that I can stretch out more comfortably.

When the bus pulls into a Jalisco station in the late evening hours I awaken from a dream about my mother's funeral. This happens each time I'm nearing Zacapu, where my mother died, where she's buried. I dreamed of my mother in a black coffin. Even in sleep I suspected something was off. My mother's coffin had been a deep gray.

At the actual wake, my grandmother wailed like a madwoman. She screamed all the way to church for the final blessing, and all the way to the cemetery and through the burial ceremony. Her shrieking made the whole ordeal intolerable for my brother and me; just as we would tire of crying, our grandmother's grief recharged our energy to start sobbing again.

The wake was held in my grandparents' living room. My mother's two weeping brothers had carried out every piece of furniture to the neighbor's house. In the center of the room, the coffin was on display with a candle lit at each corner. I sat to the side against the wall; I was the object of people's pity. Earlier in the afternoon, my grandmother had admonished me for participating in a game of tag with the boys in the neighborhood who had come to the wake with their mothers.

"What are you doing, you?" my grandmother yelled, yanking me by the arm. "Don't you know your mother is dead?"

A sympathetic woman came to my defense. "Leave him alone, comadre," she said. "He's just a child."

I was tired of sitting up in front of the hypnotic candle flames and had begun to doze off when a woman walked past me with a young boy holding on to her long black skirt.

"Is she alive?" the young boy asked.

"She's sleeping," the woman answered softly. "Do you want to see her sleeping?"

The boy nodded and the woman lifted him up for a better view.

"She's pretty," the boy said.

"Yes," the woman agreed. "She's a pretty woman. She's asleep now, waiting for God."

When the woman and child walked away I became curious. I had seen my mother lying in her coffin all afternoon, but the woman's words intrigued me. I hopped off the chair and stepped forward, standing on my toes to look inside. My mother was lying under a protective glass. She didn't look as if she were asleep at all. I became annoyed at the woman's observation—she didn't know what my mother looked like when she slept. Suddenly, a strange activity took place. Out of my mother's nostril, bubbling foam began to grow. I froze in astonishment and was quick to conclude that my mother was coming back to life.

"Look! Look!" I shouted. "She's moving!"

A few adults rushed over to see. "What is that, you?" one of them asked.

"Is she alive?" I asked, but no one heard me. In fact no one acknowledged that it had been me who had made the discovery. After a brief and subdued commotion, small pieces of white cotton had been stuffed into my mother's nostrils. I looked on in horror. Worse yet, when the glass had been temporarily removed to plug my mother's nose, a fly had snuck in. I watched it stick to the inside of the glass, its grotesque underside exposed.

*E*ven before the bus leaves the Jalisco terminal, it breaks down. A collective groan rises from those passengers who, like my father and me, have been on this journey from the beginning. The driver acts quickly, telling us that he will get us to our destinations even if he has to give us vouchers for a different bus line. He's true to his word and within the hour, everyone mutters their quick good-byes and parts ways.

My father takes the voucher and checks for the next available bus into Michoacán while I guard the luggage. I ignore the beggars and expect I'll have to get nasty with one when a young man walks up to me and surprises me with an odd request before I have time to react.

"Did you happen to see any cans left on the bus?" he asks me.

I'm attracted to him in an instant. His hair is long and wavy, his skin smooth and golden. Still, his question catches me off guard. He looks away, perhaps embarrassed that I'm staring at him.

"I collect cans, you see," he explains. "Not just any cans, but American cans. This bus came from the north, right? Did you happen to see any cans left inside?"

I become self-conscious of my sticky face and dirty shirt. When we used to take these treks down to Zacapu by car with my grandparents, my grandmother used to hand-wash our clothing in motel sinks. The clothes never dried completely by the time my grandfather woke us up to continue the journey, so she stuffed our damp clothing in plastic bags and they arrived to Zacapu smelling like piss. That's what I imagine I smell like now.

I shake my head, trying to understand his idea of an American can. All the while I begin to fantasize. I'm horny for physical contact, for fierce affection with manly strength and unrestrained force—a type of violent overpowering I have learned to demand from my lovers. I endow this body before me with that sense of predatory aggression, and I'm hoping he will act on it and claim me.

My fixed stare is enough for him to shy away, and as I watch him leave I have the urge to run and tell him that everything is fine, that I understand him and his desire to collect American cans. We all have our private pleasures. Mine are books and young men like him who wait for the buses from out of town to see what hidden treasures they bring. I want to know his name and whether he feels the same sensations for me as I do for him. I want us to seek out American cans together.

When my father arrives at that moment with a pair of onion-thin tickets in his hand, I know he has skimped again and used the voucher on tickets in second class.

"So," he says. "What's the first thing you're going to do once you get to Zacapu?"

"I never should have made this fucking trip with you!" I yell at him.

"We'll be in Michoacán by tomorrow morning," he says. "Or noon at the latest. Maybe early afternoon. Don't worry."

"You and your stupid second class bus!"

"What? Is it my fault this one broke down, too?"

"It's your fault we're on it!" I say. I walk away, forcing my father to pick up all the bags to follow me.

"It's the bus at the end!" he calls out. "The one with the yellow arrow!"

Adolescent
Mariposa

Ghost Whisper to My Lover

Don't be surprised, querido, but you're the first Mexican I've ever known who isn't a Catholic. No wonder you're fearless. But I can't say I'm much of a Catholic myself.

The Eucharist entered my body only once, on the day of my First Communion. My brother and I went through the religious ceremony one hot summer in 1984 because this was one of my mother's last wishes—that we fulfill the third of the holy Sacraments.

Usually, an entire group of children takes communion at once, after a long year of study at catechism class. But my aunt was enterprising and convinced a Sunday school teacher to make an exception for this special circumstance. The teacher squeezed the lessons into a month, after which we presented ourselves before God, the ordained priest, our chosen god-fathers, and a small congregation for the symbolic mass.

The ceremony was not particularly eventful, except that the priest insisted on changing into a more colorful tunic when my aunt asked to take pictures. He stretched out a light blue robe to display the image of the Virgin Mary at prayer, white doves hovering above her as if they were about to descend on her head. Most memorable was the day before the mass, at confession. I had always known about the confessional, a large wooden box that allows the priest to listen to a sinner's most intimate admissions without the shame of meeting eye to eye. I had been coached by *the catechism teacher for everything except the shock of finding no confessional when I entered the rectory. I looked around uncertainly.*

"Sit down, my son," the priest said. He was a short Mexican Indian wearing sandals, a trait of the Franciscan order.

I took a seat. He pulled out a second chair from behind the desk and positioned it in front of me. He sat down and bowed his head, asking me to proceed. I stuttered, mumbled, and cleared my throat repeatedly but managed to reveal what I needed to confess: use of offensive language, disrespect for my elders, masturbation, jealousy, envy, rage—the typical wrongdoings of a fourteen-year-old Catholic boy.

I didn't dwell on any details and neither did the priest ask for them. When I stepped out of the church that afternoon I was supposed to feel liberated, absolved, cleansed. But I felt none of those things as I was greeted by the blinding glare of the summer sun. Behind me the stone saints whispered among themselves the sacrilege that was my incomplete confession. I had not told the priest everything. How could I tell him that the holiness of prayer was powerless before my fury of desire for other males?—a sin, according to the Catholic Church.

I can trace back the moment I first got a taste of this lust: my childhood days in Zacapu. The neighbors from across the street were rigorously religious, the three daughters and two sons subject to the strictest of censures. They were not allowed to cuss or engage in any type of physical contact with another child, even in play. For the longest time I thought it was because of our susceptibility to contagious head lice. When the crowd of children gathered outside to shoot marbles or to play hopscotch, the mother or father stood like an apparition at a nearby window, keeping an eye on their charges. They remained invisible until one of the other children said something or did something they perceived as inappropriate. "Come inside," the voice would command from behind a curtain, and the game would suffer all of a sudden because of the surprised betrayal that an adult had been present the entire time. We could hear the children being slapped or spanked, punishment for having been exposed to the vulgarity of others.

The parents were overprotective at every moment. Once, when our family went over for dinner, we were asked politely to leave after my brother, five years old at the time, pointed out that a woman on the television screen was pregnant. But that didn't stop their children from sneaking into the second floor of our house, or to the cornfield behind the house where we engaged in sexual experimentation over the years. With the youngest daughter, who was my age, I practiced penetration, and with the oldest son, being penetrated, which I enjoyed even more.

"I must fuck you because you have no second Christian name, just a gap between your first and last names, like an opened asshole," the son would say each time, distracting me with his puzzling preamble as he pushed himself inside of me.

At the parochial school, I engaged in more child's play. During recess many of the kids hid inside an abandoned building within the school grounds, pulling underwear down to the ankles to make comparisons. This was easier for the girls, who wore regulation skirts. The boys had a belt buckle, a button, and a zipper to contend with. Our favorite game was a pissing contest, everyone standing in a row, male and female. When the boys started to dare the girls to take the small cocks into their mouths they ran out of the building. But afterward this new possibility for pleasure became my obsession, and my lover from across the street was more than willing to let me have my fill of him. Somehow these moments managed to remain untouched by the religious sovereigns who loomed above him with their codes of conduct.

Can you imagine, querido, how I'd even begin to explain to my father confessor that I was a mariposa through and through? A mariposa. You know, a homosexual.

The week before confession, the catechism teacher told us a story about a boy who took communion with an unclean soul—he had neglected to disclose the smallest of his sins, which he thought too small to merit mention to the priest. He grew up a pious Catholic, following the righteous path into adolescence, when he found his calling and became a servant for the Lord. He lived his years a respected priest, dedicated wholeheartedly to his loyal congregation. And when he died he was all but declared a saint for his devoutness and devotion. After he was buried in the sacred ground of the churchyard, his ghost began to haunt the coldest hours of the night. The new young priest was repeatedly awakened by this specter until he found the courage through the Lord to confront this abomination. He recognized the figure of the former priest and demanded that the devil behind this mockery reveal itself in its true from.

"It is I," the ghost-priest moaned. When he opened his mouth to speak he exposed the nature of his condemnation. On his tongue, the outline of that first wafer lay branded and smoking, keeping the priest's spirit from its peace. He explained his transgression to the young priest, asking him to spread the word to the members of the congregation, to every son and daughter of God, and especially to the children, that their beloved priest must now wander for all eternity chained to this earthly purgatory—a warning to all that God forgives only that which is confessed to Him through true repentance and atonement.

I walked down the church steps, keeping my secret stitched to my tongue. After the ceremony I would have no one to answer for my yearnings but myself, even if after my death I would have to lag behind that priest until the end of days, a pair of branded souls dragging the heavy burdens of their sins, like cows roaming the foggiest dawns, the first guiding the second with its dangling rosary of a tail.

Indio, 1983–88
("El Campo" Years)

As the story goes, my mother had been picking grapes along with her crew at one of the Freeman fields in the Coachella Valley. The harvest season had just begun, but already the day temperatures were uncomfortably warm. She became thirsty, nothing out of the ordinary, so she informed her coworkers that she was going down to the end of the field block to have a drink of water from the supervisor's water tank. Ten minutes passed and she hadn't returned. The grape packer grumbled: *Was she taking a drink or a vacation?* Ten more minutes went by. *Did she go home?* After half an hour, the coworkers became alarmed. *Jesús, María y José.* This absence was more than atypical; it was threatening. A quick reconnaissance confirmed that my mother was indeed missing, so the supervisor improvised a search party. When the men spread about the block in groups of threes and fours, the women huddled together in a protective circle. The foremen didn't even bother sending anyone back to work, fearing the worst when a woman disappears.

She's over here! a voice called out from the center of the sea of grapevines. *She's over here!* And a dead calm settled over the farmworkers as if the very air they breathed had frozen.

My mother was found wandering through the lush vines, incoherent, the victim of a stroke. She was taken to the Kennedy Memorial Hospital in Indio, and then eventually transferred to Eisenhower

Medical Center in Rancho Mirage, just a short drive away. When my brother and I arrived home after school, we climbed up the wooden steps and found ourselves locked out of our little home on top of the garage. We banged on the door, expecting one of our parents to come out at any moment to scold us for making such a racket. No response. Suddenly, the landlord's wife came out and waved us down. In the time we had been living next to her, she had never spoken to us even though her children came over quite often to invite us out to play. The softness of her voice was disconcerting, not at all what I imagined her sounding like after all those stories her children told us about how much she yelled at them.

"You must be strong, children," she said to us. "I have some bad news to tell you."

Her tone and diction disoriented me further. She had called us children, but she was talking to us in that polite way adults speak when they address strangers.

"Your mother has been hospitalized. Again. She suffered a small accident at work, so she won't be coming home tonight. Your father called me, and he gave me specific instructions. I will be looking after you this afternoon until one of your relatives arrives to pick you up. Please wash up before you come in."

She walked back into her house, robot-like, leaving my brother and me speechless and numb with shock. But we did what we were told. We spat-combed our hair, washed our hands and faces with the hose behind the garage, and then knocked timidly on the back door of the landlord's house. I was surprised at the size of the house. The dining room alone was larger than our entire home, and this made me feel smaller still. While we nibbled on the bland sandwiches, none of the landlord's children came to eat with us, and then the landlord's wife went on and on about her own misfortune with a broken pinky and the brief episode at the hospital that followed her traumatic incident.

"How my children cried for me," she said. "And there I was in my hospital bed, crying out for them as well. The whole family was in tears. The whole world, it seemed. But I'm so pleased to see there isn't any of that theater here."

Between bites I cursed her. And then I cursed my father for entrusting this sow with our care. And then I cursed the rest of the family for leaving us with the sow longer than we could possibly bear. Alex and I sat in those clean chairs, eating off those clean plates, refusing to let the sow see us dirty our clean faces.

Not long after her hospitalization, my mother underwent open-heart surgery to replace a defective valve. This was a long-overdue operation. An artificial valve was inserted, and it made a loud ticking noise like a clock each time it opened and closed to let the blood flush through. The thin scar of the incision trailed up between her breasts. For weeks the incessant ticking kept us from a good night's sleep in our little home on top of the garage. The sound kept my mother awake even longer. My maternal grandmother received a special visitor's visa to stay with us for a month. Up until then my older female cousin had been coming over to cook and clean for us.

As part of her therapy, my mother was given a plastic apparatus to strengthen her breathing. She blew into a small tube that sent three plastic spheres spiraling up inside a clear container. The other recommendation was exercise, and since my maternal grandmother's stay had come and gone, it was now me who guided my mother into the school grounds across the street each morning. School was out for the summer, so we paced slowly around the grassy field undisturbed, her weight on my shoulder as she leaned heavily when she stepped on her left foot. The stroke had permanently damaged one side of her body. Her left arm and leg muscles had stiffened, and the left side of her face drooped. To compensate for the spittle that spilled out of her mouth, which she couldn't close entirely, she carried a white, feminine hanky to wipe herself off each time she remembered.

And though her speech was also impaired, she insisted on these long conversations during our walks, revealing to me everything I had to know now that I was grown up enough to hear and understand them. I had just turned twelve.

"Your hateful grandfather," she said one time, "once put a gun to my head back in Bakersfield. I want you to find that gun and put it to *his* head."

"I made your father quit that band," she said on another occasion, "because of those women. They gave him pictures of themselves in the nude. I tore them all up and threw the pieces on his dinner."

"I was named after my father's first love," she told me. "She died when she was young, and your grandmother placed a curse on that name. I too will die young."

Always these confessions were followed by a long string of incoherent ramblings. I simply listened to her, collecting these odd pronouncements—what little I could comprehend through her slurred speech—like riddles to unravel in my head as I was sinking into dreams guided by the ticking of my mother's heart. I treasured them as gifts, but not as truths. I knew better since I had heard my grandmother confide in my father that my mother would slip into these trance-induced murmurings on their walks as well.

"The things she says, you," she whispered from the kitchen table. In our little home on top of the garage, everything was audible. "Does she know what she's saying?"

"The doctor said that even her brain has been affected," my father replied. "Half the time she doesn't know what's coming out of her mouth."

The surgery would only extend her life by a few months, and my father knew this, so he allowed my mother to travel back to Michoacán to be with her parents in Zacapu for the last time. Alex and I went with her.

We moved into our grandparents' house in Colonia Obrera before the end of the summer of 1982. We traveled by airplane because my mother couldn't possibly withstand the journey by bus. It was the first time any of us had been on a plane and the flight was swift and uneventful. The expense, however, had to be covered by pulling together whatever was left after the costly surgery once the Medicare had been exhausted. My father sold most of our belongings and moved in with my uncle and his family. My mother pawned her wedding ring and borrowed money from my aunts, offering up her best clothes as collateral. They even tapped into my piggy bank, using my stash of quarters to buy an old brown leather suitcase from the Goodwill Thrift Store.

When summer ended, it was clear we were not going to be returning to the United States, so by fall my mother enrolled my brother and me in the primary school Vasco de Quiroga, named after that great missionary advocate of the Purépecha. We were held back a grade because, as the director of the school explained it, American education was not as advanced as the Mexican system. Indeed, during math my classmates were already doing fractions and I had never been exposed to them before. But the director took a liking to me immediately because I was the son of a band member of Dinastía. Six years ago, the band had held a fundraising concert at the school. With some of the money raised, the director bought a small sound system and microphone—the same ones he still used to shout out marching instructions at the student body as we prepared for the annual Independence Day parade in September. He also liked showing off his English in front of the other kids. Each time I strained to understand what he was trying to say, but his pantomiming was helpful.

The director may have been impressed by our presence at his school, but not the other kids. We had only been away from México a few years and already we were considered foreigners—gringos, pochos, gavachos—Americanos. During recess my brother immediately gravitated toward me, hiding behind me from the taunting of his peers. The last time he did that was when he was diagnosed with an allergy to airborne pollen back in Thermal. The doctor suggested that he wear sunglasses for a few weeks, and my mother picked out an outrageous green-tinted pair at Goodwill. He was fine at first until one of the teachers saw him and called him Joe Cool. After that he came directly toward me at recess to stand inside my shadow. I felt just as helpless then as I did at Vasco de Quiroga in general, unable to offer him a word of comfort, not when I could have used one for myself—I, too, was designated the school freak. But our days in Za-capu were numbered. While my brother and I practiced the march-ing drills in the afternoons, my mother's health kept deteriorating. At night, her groans filled the house with an anxiety that gave every-one nightmares.

My mother died in Zacapu on September 12, at the age of thirty-one. She died sitting between her parents in a car en route to the hospital in Morelia, the state capital, after complaining of intoler-able chest and stomach pains. I remember my grandmother saying one morning after the funeral that she had dreamed she was having a long conversation with my mother.

"What did you talk about?" I asked, hoping to latch on to some last word or phrase that could fill the void of her having gone with-out a good-bye.

"What does it matter now?" my grandmother replied. "She's gone. Dreamed words are empty words."

I didn't press her any further; my mind filled with the image of my grief-stricken grandmother at the church and at the cemetery, drunk and crying the sorrow of a thousand lungs—a spine-tingling shrill that still makes me shudder whenever I remember that solemn day. In fact, my grandmother had been such a distracting presence during the whole of the funeral that people kept quiet about the priest. Not until after the wake did people began to murmur, and even then they kept their voices low. When we had arrived at the church with my mother's coffin for the last rites, the priest was nowhere to be found. After much waiting, the congregation growing uncomfortably rest-less, my father and the other pallbearers broke into the adjacent building, a small cottage, where the priest was found in a deep sleep. People said that my father throttled the priest out of bed and had to be held back. When the priest finally came up to the altar, his hair un-combed and his frock unkempt, he delivered the service under the pressure of my father's threat that if he screwed up he would kill him. Everyone in church that morning saw that the priest was hung over.

During the wake was also the only time I ever saw my maternal grandfather cry. My grandfather had always been a giant to me: tall, strong, and slim, he had worked as a bracero for many years until he married. After the birth of his first child, my mother, he settled down in Zacapu, where he eventually found a job at the mercado bringing in cargo—a job he kept well into his old age. He was a quiet, unassuming, and gentle man whom my brother and I loved dearly because he was nothing like our father's father. Our mother's mother, in contrast, was nothing like our beloved grandmother back in California. Our Purépecha grandmother was gentile and soft-spoken, with an incomparable sense of humor. During the wake my brother and I hid away from the rest of the mourners by going up on the roof, where my grandparents always kept chickens we were forbidden to name because they would each end up in the cooking pot. There we cried privately. My brother kept repeating, "We came here so she could die." I couldn't contradict his statement. Suddenly we heard someone climb the cement steps. We were standing behind the chicken coop so our grandfather didn't see us. He looked out toward the highest peak in the mountains, "el cerro del Tecolote," as he burst into tears, blowing his nose into a handkerchief before going down into the house again. My brother and I looked at each other and cried again. My little brother Alex was only ten years old.

My father, my uncle and my Purépecha grandmother flew down from California in time for the funeral. It was the first and only time any of them had been on a plane as well. I would hear many years later how my grandmother had to sit with a towel around her head because she didn't want to look out the window. And when she had to use the bathroom, she got down on all fours, expecting to crawl to the back of the plane.

"I was so embarrassed, you," my uncle told us. "But then the flight attendant came and guided her to the bathroom and back. But she still wouldn't take the towel off her head."

"She looked like a hijacking hostage," my father added.

We stayed through the novena, the nine days of prayer after the burial. My father was kind to us, embracing and kissing us frequently. I enjoyed that attention. So it wasn't hard for my brother and me to make up our minds to return with him to the United States.

My mother's family was furious. They didn't want us to return to that monster back in California. My mother had told them how he used to beat us and how he had threatened to strike her. But my father insisted.

"They're my sons," he told them firmly.

He told us the same thing when we slept together in the same bed the night before our return, my brother and I lying on either side of him. In a surprising gesture, he opened up a large Bible and showed us the illustrations of heaven and hell.

"Your mother is here now," he said as he pointed to a drawing of cottony clouds inhabited by pale-faced, golden-haired angels with white wings. God was depicted sitting on a throne. His gigantic body dwarfed the angels to the size of pigeons, and instead of a head, a yellow ball of light was perched on his neck, as if his face had caught on fire.

"You're my sons," he said to us. "It's the three of us now. We have to stay together forever."

When we left Zacapu, we left our mother buried at the panteón, but we also left Vasco de Quiroga, where we didn't fit in, and we left the corrugated tin roof of our room in our grandparents' house, where raindrops sounded like marbles dropping. We took the train back to Mexicali. The journey was long, but it was more relaxing than the bus. As I tried to sleep on my seat, I kept getting nervous whenever the train passed through a series of mountain tunnels in Jalisco. I kept my eyes fixed on my father as he vanished for seconds at each blackout, each time expecting him not to reappear when the cabin came to light.

Within days of returning to California, we went to live with our paternal grandparents in Indio since my father concluded that he could not raise his sons alone. But very soon after that, he decided it was time to find another wife. The adults in the family supported my father's decision. He was a man, after all, and he needed someone to care for him; he was falling to pieces without a wife, they said, pointing out that in the few months that my mother was gone his drinking had worsened. Once he was even arrested for brawling on the streets. The phone rang the morning after my father didn't come home after going out with friends. My grandfather answered it.

"You're where?" my grandfather gasped. "And why?"

After a lengthy silence, my grandfather yelled into the phone: "Then walk your ass home!"

My father walked through the desert all the way from the detention center. When he arrived he looked hungover, filthy, and bloody. He showered and refused to talk about what had happened, though my grandfather more than gladly filled in the details for us, as a warning against drinking and rowdy behavior.

"What kind of example is that for your sons, you?" my grandfather declared self-righteously.

It pained me to see my father lectured in front of me, his head down like a shamed child, but I began to speak to him with my grandfather's tone as well because it seemed to be the only way to make him listen.

The next time my father was out drinking late and the phone rang, I answered.

"I need you to pick me up," my father said.

"Are you in jail again?" I asked, furiously.

My father chuckled. "No," he said. "I'm at Ilario's in Coachella. Come pick me up, son."

I took the car keys and drove to Ilario's house just a short distance away. Ilario was one of my father's best friends and a former musician as well. I was still learning how to drive, but I reasoned this was an emergency, and the fact that I could take the back roads where there was very little traffic gave me courage. My hands trembled on the steering wheel. I drove up, greeted Ilario, picked up my father, and then drove back. On the way home my father was quiet, and I would have kept my mouth shut as well but then he spoke up in that sentimental way that he talks when he's drunk.

"I've always looked forward to this moment," he said.

I ignored him.

"I've always looked forward to the moment," he repeated, "when my son would be grown up enough to pick me up in a car."

I started crying. "What kind of pleasure does this give you, calling in the middle of the night because you're drunk?" I said. I didn't look at him during the long silence that followed.

Every week it was the same story: my father got drunk, my grandfather threw fits, and my brother and I had to listen to the scolding from our beds, pretending to be asleep when our father stumbled into the room because watching him cry was intolerable. Behind the safety of my eyelids I cursed my father, wishing it had been he who had died, and not my mother.

The helplessness of adolescence was maddening. I began to wish that I were dead, released from this anxiety that kept me up at nights. Once, when an earthquake shook the rest of the household awake, I thought that my own rage had caused it. Since I now slept in the living room, no longer willing to share a room with my father, I was acquiring these special gifts: the gift of becoming as still and breathless as the couch, the gift of finding holes in the shadows that opened up into distant worlds, and the gift of breaking the earth apart with the destructive energy of my heavy thoughts. And there, beneath the dining table, was my grandfather's shotgun secured to the underside of the wood. I also had the gift of floating my animus through the dark to send back reports of the shapes in the weapon — the flatness of the heel, the curve of the trigger, the journey of the shaft, and the curious ring of the barrel.

For everyone else, escape came easily. A brief and devastating period followed in which people walked away to live their own lives, leaving my brother and me behind to bear our orphan status like identification labels on unclaimed luggage.

Our recently divorced uncle left us, fleeing to México to avoid paying child support. Our oldest cousin took his place, but then he left us, off to elope with his beloved. Even our grandparents' bachelor son, who we all thought would never marry, finally did. He left us, vanishing with his new bride into the anonymous streets of the Coachella Valley. He became more of a rumor, and it was something of a novelty, like sightings of Elvis, if any one of us ever saw him. And then our father left us.

When I left Indio, it was to convalesce in Mexicali after my nervous breakdown, after weeks of missing school and weeks of trying to convince my grandfather that I wasn't well. Couldn't he see it in my eyes, cracked like glass? Couldn't he see it on my skin, yellow and tough like dirty wax? In Mexicali I stayed in my aunt's old house, raking the leaves in the mornings, watering the plants in the afternoon. She kept an eye on me through the window. I once overheard her talking through the fence to a neighbor who was curious about my sudden appearance.

"He's been through so much," my aunt said. "His mother died. His father left him. Of course anyone would go soft in the head."

"And how long are you looking after him?" the neighbor asked.

"As long as it takes," she said. "He's my brother's child, but I owe his mother at least that."

But healed or not, my grandfather soon came down to get me because I didn't need a sane mind, just a good pair of hands, to work the grape harvest when summer came around.

In the summers, my brother and I joined our grandparents in the fields, picking grapes, toiling under the same conditions that had defeated my mother. In the fields, our faces hid behind bandannas for protection from sunburn and from excessive exposure to the pesticides and sulfur. Sweaty and thick with dust, they were stripped of expression by the end of the days. And every morning I woke up at dawn with a sharp pain in my throat as I suppressed the grief of having to regress to a life under my grandfather's rule.

But this was home, this government-subsidized cinderblock

apartment of the Fred Young Farm Labor Camp, commonly referred to as "el campo." In the 1970s it was an idyllic community since the housing was new, the lawns were fresh with watered grass, the trees were pruned to matching cookie-cutter proportions, the walls were as white and clean as canvases, and the rows of front doors alternated colors between red and blue—a patriotic display for a neighborhood of Mexican farmworkers. By the time my family moved there in the early 1980s, "el campo" had gained a reputation as a thriving nest for thieves, drug dealers, drug addicts, and gangs. Every night the sound of gunfire made holes in the sky, followed by the wailing of police cars and ambulances. Watching a knife fight in the middle of the street was an alternative spectacle to the television and my family kneeled shoulder to shoulder on the couch and peeked through the curtains, knowing our neighbors were doing the same because suddenly all the living room lights went off to help us hide like an audience in a theater.

The apartments were also infested with cockroaches. One of the first suggestions my grandmother made when we moved in was to make sure the roaches crawled out of the cereal before we poured in the milk. The second suggestion was to sleep with cotton in our ears so that the tiny roaches didn't crawl in at night and cause an infection.

In the late 1980s a wall was constructed that divided the land between "el campo" and a large, barren lot that had always been used as a meeting place by the young people showing off their customized cars. Not long afterward the citizenry of "el campo" heard the invasion of construction crews erecting building structures. The commotion was heard, not seen, because the cinderblock wall obstructed the view, which was really designed to spare the new neighbors a glimpse of "el campo." That meant two things: that the buildings next door would not be low-income government-subsidized housing, and that "el campo" was there to stay, and still stands, sheltering the ever-present farmworking community of the Coachella Valley.

By this time, at the age of fourteen, I began wearing glasses even though I had needed corrective lenses since elementary school. Somehow I got by, squinting, asking for clarification, and sitting in the front rows of the classroom. But as a freshman in high school I realized my usual tactics were useless because my vision had worsened. In algebra class, the math teacher worked out the problems on the blackboard, explaining the process step by step, and I could only see line after line of chicken scratches. She was so methodical in the way she calculated complex equations that I knew I had to speak up or risk losing the chance to witness the marvel of her multiplying and dividing letters and numbers.

My grandparents couldn't believe I wanted glasses since only older people like themselves wore them. None of their other grandchildren needed them. In fact, none of their grown-up children used them either.

"Are you sure?" they kept asking.

Luckily, my grandmother's insurance at the packinghouse could cover the expenses. My grandfather pulled me out of school one day to take me to the eye doctor, a balding man who made me uncomfortable each time his freckled head came near me during the examination. Each time that he adjusted the machine mask that looked like a mechanical butterfly over my face, I could hear his wheezing. I held my own breath in those instances, as if I were the prey hiding out from the predator whiffing out the trail of my scent. At the end of the exam the optometrist expressed much surprise that a person with my degree of myopia had never used glasses.

"What have you been looking at in the mirror all this time?" he joked.

My grandfather picked out my frames because he said he had all the experience in the matter. Indeed, the wall stared out at me like a coliseum of bespectacled invisible men. The frames he chose were alarmingly similar to the ones he himself wore, but I didn't object. I was grateful I was going to be able to see more clearly. And then he reminded me of my grandmother's suggestion to get those slightly tinted lenses that darkened when exposed to the sun, just like the ones she had.

A week later the glasses were ready and again my grandfather drove me to the optometrist in his old pickup.

"Maybe you shouldn't read as much," he suggested as he entered the mall parking lot.

Placing the glasses on my face disoriented me immediately. I had the sensation of standing at the edge of a cliff, and since I also suffered from a mild case of acrophobia, the feeling made my heart flutter. I looked around me in the mall, the lighting too bright, the people too exposed. As soon as I stepped out into natural light, the lenses began to darken. When I watched my grandfather behind the wheel of the pickup, I traced the definitions of his age and the damage of his numerous strokes on his face—wrinkles, flabby chin, the squinting right eye and its fan of deep grooves reaching out from its corner. He had been dyeing his hair, eyebrows, and mustache for years now to hide the outgrowths of white. The job was painfully obvious.

When we drove into "el campo," slowing down through the enclosed streets, I noticed people looking back, men especially. And for the first time I recognized the look of mutual attraction from a distance.

My grandmother looked no different than before because she always had the habit of coming too close to my face when she whispered a secret, looking into my eyes, not my ear. This was how she looked at me when she told me that it was my grandfather who had initiated my father's alcoholism. I asked her how that could be. She told me that each day after a hard day's work in the fields, my father and my uncle came home to a can of soda until my grandfather insisted that they start drinking beer because they weren't children anymore. One week is all it took to get them hooked, and not long after that they became the men that my grandfather wanted them to be—vulnerable and under his control. When she spoke with her gaze fixed on me that way, I knew that what passed between us was the sacred truth of our family's history.

The next morning I put on my glasses, looking forward to all of my classes, and to discovering the blackboard all over again. But before I even climbed onto the bus I was met with another surprise.

Up to that morning, I had been getting on the bus while greeting the driver with a smile. It was an apologetic smile for her having to pick up a rowdy group of kids who pushed and shoved their way in like a cattle stampede during roundup time at the corral. Through my bad eyes, her face looked blurry, scratched out. But I knew there was a face there by the frontal view of her yellow hair. And I could sense her warm welcome.

When my turn came to go up, I expected to see a clearer picture of what I had always imagined—a young woman with a pretty face. But my smile melted away as soon as I was greeted with an old, tired woman who bit severely into an unfriendly frown. She didn't even look at me at all. Her eyes stared right through me as if I were made of glass, as if her eyes were made of glass—the non-functional marbles in the sockets of a plastic doll.

My four years of high school were spent locked up inside "el campo." I became a voracious reader and television-watcher, keeping to myself at such alarming extremes that I became invisible. My invisibility provided the perfect protection against harm of any sort. I walked to and from school past the gangsters as silently as a breeze, so disassociated from their tattoos and lingo that even they couldn't find a place for me in their lines of vision. My grandfather continued to humiliate those around him, except for me, because I didn't say a word; I simply obeyed. I spent days and nights reading in the corner of the rooms or watching television with the volume turned so low I would surprise my grandmother when she thought she was bringing the clean linen into an empty room. In the fields, even the supervisor was intrigued by me—the sullen young man who, unlike the

rest of his workers, never complained or joked or laughed, but kept
to his task like an after-image, elusive and quickly vanishing from
sight and mind.

"He's kind of quiet, isn't he?" I heard the supervisor comment to
my grandfather.

"He doesn't cause trouble," my grandfather replied.

I withdrew into books, which I collected on the bookshelf that
went with me wherever I moved. It was the same bookshelf my parents had bought for me at the now-defunct Zody's. Books provided
me with an escape, like an inter-dimensional porthole. I began to
envision different environments and, more importantly, to imagine
myself within them. They became my substitute homes. As a reader
I preferred books whose descriptive pages contrasted with my real
life: I sought out fictions taking place in other lands at other times,
with concerns so far removed from my own that if I could have been
magically transported there I would appear as a different person
altogether, not the person who moved about in the shadows like
a fleeting flash of light. But therein lay the problem with my con-
nection to books. Deep down inside I suspected that I would never
become that different person, and that I'd always be me no matter
where I went or what I did.

*A*lways a resourceful man, my grandfather encouraged my brother
and me to stay in school for the simple reason that we were entitled
to a monthly social security check due to my mother's death. Since
he became our legal guardian, the money was used for household expenses. And as long we were enrolled in school during the academic
year, we could still join our family in the grape fields during the
summers, generating additional income. That was the huge fallout
between my brother and my grandfather when my brother dropped
out of high school, just as all of our older cousins had done. He
had followed the same pattern: skipping a day at first, then missing
days at a time until he vanished from the school roster altogether.
Angered at the loss of that regular income, my grandfather sent

my brother to live with my father, finally shattering the small unit that used to be my family in our little home on top of the garage. Not long after that, my father moved his new family back to México. My brother went with him. Neither of them returned to live in the United States again, though for years they kept coming back to work the grape harvest in the summers.

I grew closer to my grandmother during my high school years. At four-foot-eleven, she always wore her hair short and refused to wear dresses, though she appreciated costume jewelry and collected earrings with as much passion as she collected pants. She never went to church but she considered herself devoutly Catholic. When we were younger she listened to the radio service and when the preacher's voice pleaded that listeners connect with the word of God through the speakers, she did so and pressed her hands against the radio if my grandfather wasn't looking. Now she simply kept pictures of saints around the house. Her pride and joy, however, was a certificate she bought at a church in Mexicali and prominently displayed in the living room.

"With that," she explained as she pointed out the framed piece of paper—a large white sheet with a bad picture of the Pope presiding over an open-air mass, our family name clumsily penciled in on a designated line, "every time the Pope says mass, our entire family is remembered in his blessings."

My grandmother also played the harmonica skillfully, but she rarely played it. She was very private about it. In fact I had to catch her in the act of blowing a few notes into the mouthpiece when she was alone in her room. The harmonica, like my grandfather's accordion and my father's guitar, disappeared mysteriously without a trace.

My grandmother called my grandfather Satanás, Matusalén, and Diablocrú—a favorite expression of my uncle's—behind his back. She still called me Estuche, "Tuchi" for short, a childhood nickname she had given me and which only she used. It meant "slipcase"—I was her slipcase in which she kept those precious eyes, her glasses, through which she saw the world a little better. My brother Alex was simply Beneficios, "Benny" for short, because his birth and hospital stay had been fully covered by medical benefits.

Between the two of us, my grandmother and I learned to laugh at my grandfather's eccentricities. We could hear him coming because he announced himself through his whistling or his farting. My grandfather was aging rapidly, his health weakening from the high blood pressure and diabetes, and his attempts at asserting power and control were the stuff of comedy, as silly as the tattoo of the naked cartoon woman on his shoulder. He secured the protective gate at the front door each evening at seven, locking us in until the next morning because only he had a key. He would turn off the television when he wanted to, even if the rest of us were still watching from the couch. He turned off the ringer on the phone so that no calls were ever announced. He insisted on cutting our hair despite his failing eyesight, the sharp scissors clipping dangerously close to the tops of our ears, my sideburns cropped unevenly.

"He might as well do it blindfolded," my grandmother quipped.

My grandfather also had a bizarre fascination with amputating the tails of cats. He would lure a neighborhood cat into the apartment, subduing it with affection until he could coax it onto the cutting board, and then he'd bring down the cleaver, watching the stunned animal rocket out through the front door as he stood over the severed tail in a fit of uncontrollable laughter. My grandmother was also party to this cruelty, helping him ensnare the unsuspecting felines. Two of our own cats, Maurilio and Estanilaus—"Maui" and "Tani"—also fell victims to the chopping block. They paraded around the apartment looking like a common alley cat version of the lynx. Only the orange-striped tabby my brother had jokingly named Spot, a name that stuck, was spared because he resembled a graceful tiger cub. My grandfather left him intact so that he could show him off at the swap meet as he walked him on a leash. Such respect was never granted to any other animal, however, especially if the harmless creature had wronged my grandfather.

"Here," he said to me one afternoon, handing me a piece of green

Steno pad notepaper and a pen. "Write on it: *I'm dead because I shit on people's gardens.* Big letters."

"I don't understand," I said, puzzled by the odd sentence.

"You don't have to understand," he assured me. "Just write it."

I did, giving him back the completed assignment. I had forgotten entirely about the note, dismissing it as one of my grandfather's eccentricities until there was a knock on the back door. One of the neighbors peered sullenly at me through the glass window. I recognized him as the man my grandparents had nicknamed "Kanguro"—kangaroo—because when he walked he lifted his knees up as if he was climbing stairs. When I swung the door open, I immediately recognized the green piece of paper in his hand. The blood rushed to my face as I expected him to demand an explanation for this note, but instead, he said to me in a calm and somber voice: "I found this on top of my cat. Some bastard killed him. And since I can't read, can you tell me what this says?"

My grandfather did all of the cooking, yet another way to assume control. My grandmother never objected to this arrangement because she herself couldn't cook. In fact, her few attempts made me appreciate my grandfather's cooking even more. She preferred to work with soil, as a farmworker or in the garden. Afterward, she loved to enjoy her Coors, and belched with satisfaction when she threw away the empty can. While I was in "el campo," my grandfather and I took care of the light cleaning while my grandmother went to work at the packinghouse during the year. We all worked together at the grape harvest in the summers. My grandfather, now in his sixties, was receiving disability insurance until his retirement pension kicked in, though my grandmother said that if he had known about that earlier, he would have shot himself in the foot at twenty-one.

My grandfather was familiar with Filipino cuisine; he didn't like Mexican food much and rarely prepared it. He had learned Filipino cooking as a young man when he lived and worked in a labor camp occupied exclusively by men. As the story goes, one day the Filipino cook fell ill, and the boss asked the men if any of them had any experience in the kitchen. My grandfather, never one to lose an opportunity to get away from hard labor, volunteered to help until the cook recuperated. Well, my grandfather turned out to be such a promising apprentice that he was kept in the kitchen for the remaining workdays of the season, absorbing the cook's culinary techniques. My grandfather respected his own skill so much that when we went grocery shopping he refused to skimp. He criticized those who rolled their carts into the economy aisle, which was a flood of canned goods with yellow labels.

"Cheat the government, but never cheat your hunger," he used to say. Another one of his mottos was: "The biggest sin to the body is denying it good food."

My grandparents never gave me a personal allowance, but I didn't miss it; I had become a recluse, preferring to hide inside my books. Each weekend I went with my grandmother to Goodwill, where she would buy our second-hand clothes and my twenty-five-cent paperbacks with titles like *Death in the Nile, Jaws, The Last Unicorn, Coma, Flowers in the Attic,* and *Valley of the Dolls.* My aunt had shown us how to replace the price tags using a nail clipper so that we bought the used clothing at even cheaper prices. Afterward we'd go into the discount warehouse to stock up on Dolly Madison pies and cakes for my grandmother, who had an incurable sweet tooth that annoyed my grandfather because her blood sugar level remained normal.

"Indigenous blood," he used to say with envy.

The top of the refrigerator always had three boxes of cereal: Corn Flakes for me, Coco Puffs and Fruity Pebbles for my grandmother.

Alone and bored with my grandparents, I concentrated on schoolwork, which wasn't difficult without distractions. My grandparents spent their afternoons cultivating an impressive herb garden, and spent the evenings watching novelas on the Spanish station. We ate our meals in silence. Every once in a while my grandfather mentioned some uninteresting piece of gossip about the neighbors or about one of our relatives. The mood over dinner was usually passive, our faces turned toward the fish tank my grandmother kept in the center of the table. During summers she placed aspirin tablets in the cats' water dish because she was positive they too suffered from heat-wave headaches, and she dropped ice cubes into the tank so that the fish wouldn't overheat in the warm water. There was one fish in particular she was fond of, a goldfish that had grown so fat for the tank that it couldn't turn around and only floated back and forth, facing my grandfather's side of the table. My grandmother named it Chiquito.

"One of these days, you," my grandfather would threaten, "I'm going to fry Chiquito and put him on a bed of rice."

"We'll see about that," my grandmother snapped, overprotective of her pet fish.

I was caught in the middle of the occasional banter, my eyes sleepy over the plate as the food was overwhelmed by the aromas of the herb garden. I had been doing exactly that the day my grandfather announced, "I guess Chiquito found himself a girlfriend, you."

We all looked into the tank to find a drowned rat drifting in the water with its snout pointing toward the surface.

Seizing the opportunity for a comeback, my grandmother said, "Why don't you have *that* on your bed of rice."

$\mathcal{R}$iding the bus to school from "el campo" was an exercise in survival. The farmworker kids kicked, slapped, and shoved their way in to be the first to occupy the back seats. From the back a kid could defend himself more successfully from flying objects thrown around at random to strike any target. Plus, sitting in the back meant getting off last, securing protection from getting hit by the kids who spat out the windows as the first bodies walked down the sidewalk parallel to the parked bus. The bus driver had long since given up trying to instill order, somehow drowning out the noise as she drove a crowded vehicle with kids cussing and flipping the bird to every passing car.

I only remember the bus getting quiet once. Since "el campo" was located in the middle of farming territory, the bus had to pass the grape fields, the lettuce fields, the carrot fields, and the orange groves en route to the school. During the lettuce season, the farmworkers concentrated on their tasks, backs bent and asses up in the air. No one on the bus pointed them out, distracted by all the commotion, or so I believed. Then one morning as the bus passed the same scene, one of the lettuce pickers stood upright, turned his body toward our direction, and waved from side to side until the bus turned the corner. The noise simmered down, surprising even the bus driver. The noise picked up again, but somehow I sensed that others were feeling exactly as I was at that moment, saddened by that gesture of recognition by an anonymous figure in the field—somebody's father or uncle or brother or friend.

By the time I was a senior in high school, the other "el campo" kids acknowledged me as the smart one. "Schoolboy," they named me. I was the oldest of the bunch. Most of the kids of "el campo" dropped out of school by their sophomore year, or were removed from school by their parents who needed an extra body generating an income in the fields. At fourteen this was legal, as long as the former student pursued an independent course of study. As the silent and docile Schoolboy, I gained a level of respect and I wasn't harassed on the bus. I kept to myself, a book opened in front of me to give myself space and distance from the ruckus.

At the high school I attended all students were tracked according to academic achievement. I was enrolled in most of the college prep courses; "el campo" kids were mainly taking basic ed, taught by the men who also coached the soccer, swimming, and football teams. Still, many of them struggled with the work, and a few even came to me for help. That is how I met my first lover.

Gerardo had also lived in Thermal at one time, attending the same elementary school I did, which is how I first knew him. He was a self-labeled cholo, a tough kid who wore khaki pants and a white T-shirt all year long. My only exchange with him in Thermal was in the boys' bathroom. I was walking in just as he was walking out, zipping his pants, when he leaned his head over to spit in my ear, then yelled out, "Whore!"

I had been too intrigued by the word to dwell on the saliva ooz-ing out of my ear. I had wanted to turn around just then to ask for the spelling of the word because I wanted to look up the definition in the dictionary.

At the high school in Indio, Gerardo had not changed in appear-ance though he was taller. He insisted on combing his hair back even though the cholo look wasn't as popular at that school as it had been back in Thermal.

I was shocked when I saw him enter my social studies class for the first time. Gerardo still looked like a bully. But to my surprise, he was quiet, respectful, and when he sat in the desk next to mine, he looked over and gave me a heads-up gesture of recognition. I re-turned the gesture, timidly.

After a week, I suspected Gerardo's days in that upper-level class were numbered. He spent most of the time sketching lowriders in the pages of his notebook. The teacher, somehow intimidated by this odd-looking tough guy in the back, ignored him. For the most part I ignored him as well, until he threw a note on my desk asking if he could copy my homework. I thought then, here it is, the reason he was being nice to me, nodding to me each morning as we sat down in the back of the class. To keep him at bay I let him copy that and any other assignment he needed as well.

Gerardo must have survived that first month because I supplied him with answers, even during quizzes and tests. But then came the challenge: an essay. I didn't react to the announcement, knowing he would be exposed suddenly, and if I was lucky, removed from the class. But Gerardo did react, and he came up to me during lunch break to request some tutoring.

"I'll pay you," he said when I declined.

I interpreted the offer as a sign of desperation, and I agreed to it, only because this former bully was now at my mercy.

Gerardo lived in Penn West, a neighborhood that was located

behind "el campo" and was known as a more severe high-crime area. We agreed to meet at my home because his was overcrowded and he didn't want his brothers to see he was actually hitting the books for a change. I also learned that he had been put in an upper-level social studies class because the basic and general classes were already over-flowing with students. He said the administration was waiting for someone to drop out and make room, but I suspected the dropout they were waiting for was Gerardo.

Gerardo was full of surprises. On our first session, as we sat on my bed with the books opened, notebooks and pens also spread out on the comforter, he leaned over suddenly and kissed me on the cheek.

"Did you like that?" he asked.

I thought it was a trick, an attempt to make me provoke him into some violent outburst. He then pulled out a small vial from his pocket. Cocaine. I was stunned.

I was no stranger to what cocaine looked like. Some of the more troubled "el campo" kids were frequent users, so bold as to snort in the back of classrooms. They'd boast about it on the bus, and as proof of their bravado they would pull out empty vials from their pockets, or dare others to snort the rest of the powder on the bumpy ride home. But most of the time the tough guys puffed on pot, rolling the joints on their thighs as we waited for the bus.

Kissing Gerardo back was a risk, but I took it, expecting this would have to be a secret affair, like all the others. He unzipped his pants, pulled out his erection, and then guided my head toward it. He unzipped my pants to reciprocate. Soon we had the weekly routine down: We snorted the cocaine. We worked on our reports. We had sex.

I was no stranger to sex with men, but Gerardo was the first who was my age. Up to that point I had been experimenting with closeted older men I met working in the fields. They spotted me and latched on to me after work when they saw me walking down "el campo" streets, courting me as they would a girl, with low-voiced sweet talk and coy eyebrows, all of it performed clandestinely since they might have girlfriends or wives. I didn't mind the falseness of the arrangement—the ersatz affection and the discreet rendezvous that took me to the privacies of beds, shoddy couches, or even the backseats of cars. I was young, sexually driven, and hungering for attention in ways I never felt before.

During my first sexual experience with a grown man, I never felt any sense of shame. He was one of the foremen at the grape fields, his hair shoulder length and his shirt neatly tucked into his khaki pants. When he inspected the workers, he lingered with our group, chatting up my father or my uncle, who was our designated packer. I suspected he stalled at the end of the row to wait for me to walk up with a box of freshly packed grapes. I knew he desired me by the way he stared. I was fourteen at the time; he must have been in his thirties. I have since learned to differentiate the stubble on a face: the coarser the hair, the older the man. When he pulled me out of the group, nobody questioned his intent. It was not out of the ordinary for foremen to single out workers for one reason or another. He made me stamp the company identification number on every packed box along the edge of a field. As I worked my way down I was actually moving opposite the flow of the crew, so that when I reached the end I could barely make out the moving bodies. What I did see clearly was the foreman driving up the dusty avenue to pick me up as he had promised. But he didn't let me climb into the truck before embracing me first. Not a single word was spoken as he undid my shirt and my pants. I didn't object to his mouth running down my chest and biting down on my nipples. I ejaculated as soon as he entered me, both of us pressed against the seat of the truck. The smell of layers of sulfur and sweat that had permeated the seat covering made me nauseous, so I held my breath until he came. We got into the truck and drove back to the crew. The stickiness between my ass cheeks and the scent of my own shit bothered me and excited me for the rest of the afternoon. And though I wanted this encounter to happen again, the grape harvest came to a close without him coming around to even look at me again.

Sex with another man seemed so natural to me, the contact so necessary. Certainly the pleasure was rewarding, but so was the transgression—the only time I felt in control, even as I let the men do with me what they wanted, with whatever force. Even Gerardo was not a gentle lover, locking his teeth on my neck at the moment of his drug-heightened orgasm. And I accepted this momentary lapse into violence as our journey away from ourselves and into fantasy. I looked forward to losing myself in the fury of sex, in the struggle of it, in its bruise of a kiss. Stripping myself of clothes was like stripping myself of problems, so I readily sought those sessions of escape.

The more Gerardo and I saw of each other in private, the less we communicated in public. Even in class I stopped looking at him, afraid that my glance might betray the desire I had for him, and which he fulfilled. My grandparents didn't approve much of Gerardo coming into the apartment, but accepted that he was there to do homework. He in turn was polite, charming even, tapping into my grandfather's social skills with conversation about the weather, the latest world events, and car maintenance.

But I never fantasized that our relationship would go on forever. Nothing ever did, not in "el campo," not in my life. Besides, romantic relationships between men were an impossibility if you weren't really a homosexual. Gerardo never said he was gay, and neither did any of the men I had been sleeping with. And for the longest time I doubted that I was gay myself because this identity was never talked about by any of us or even recognized in the secrecy of the dark bedrooms.

"I'm leaving school," Gerardo announced one afternoon. We were lying on the floor in our underwear. We never had sex on the bed because I was afraid my grandmother might spot us twisting around on the sheets as she worked in the garden.

"Are you going away?" I asked. Gerardo had smooth skin with dimples above his ass cheeks that I enjoyed inserting my tongue into.

"Maybe," he said. "But either way I won't need any more tutoring."

"I guess not," I said.

"I'm going to help my family out. You know how it is."

"I'll see you in the grape?" I asked.

"Nah," he said. "I'm dealing this." He waved the empty vial in the air.

"Oh," I said softly. He moved closer to me and we had sex again before he left for the last time.

I accepted Gerardo's good-bye without much of a struggle. Over the years I had been saying good-bye to the people I loved. Gerardo left school and left me. I made no effort to seek him out or to call him. I went back to school the next day knowing there would be an empty desk next to mine at social studies class, and that these other students, most of them white and in college prep classes, would have no clue about what had transpired between these two brown kids who sat in the back of the classroom.

I saw Gerardo only one other time after we parted ways. A few years after graduating from high school I was visiting my grandparents. I drove my grandmother to the swap meet and I saw him there, directing traffic with a red flag at the parking lot. Gerardo stood tall, seemed chunkier, and sported a goatee. I knew he had recognized me as well. I parked the car. He moved on to the next available space and flagged down another vehicle.

For some odd reason, my parents had never talked to me about puberty and all its complications and had simply let me stumble in the dark with my discoveries. The closest they ever got to communicating any form of sex education was when they left a pair of pornographic magazines on their bed back in our little home on top of the garage. Without any explanation the explicit pages waited for my brother and me. Clearly it was an invitation, but once we exhausted our eyesight with these images, there was no follow-up discussion, so the act remained a dirty secret among us.

The year I turned eleven my father was still working for the construction crews because many of them hired labor off the streets and paid non-taxable wages in the form of cold cash. Occasionally the crew was hired for a project in Palm Springs. Palm Springs was a haven for retired actors and well-meaning debutantes who championed such causes as wildlife sanctuaries and who organized golf tournaments for charity. The Coachella Valley got to hear all about the rich folks through the evening news and Gloria Greer's "Stars of the Desert." Featured in her segment were costume balls, barbecue fundraisers, and the rare interview with the likes of Florence "Mrs. Brady" Henderson.

At one time or another everyone in the Valley knew of someone who crossed paths with a famous name, especially if that someone worked at the plush hotels or on the luxury links. Or in construction, like my father.

"My father did some renovating for Bob Hope," I bragged to a friend.

Not to be outdone he proudly replied, "My father fixed a driveway for Kirk Douglas."

Among the countless celebrities who inhabited the Palm Springs area was Liberace, the flamboyant entertainer with the trademark candelabra and outlandish outfits. He was easy to imitate. I simply threw a comforter or an unzipped sleeping bag over my shoulders and let it drag like a train, Lady Di wedding dress style. I never mastered the walk across the carpet in a pair of my mother's high heels, so I wobbled all over my pretend stage.

What attracted me to Liberace was the way he got away with the whole theater of his presentation: mink, rings, makeup, and a hairdo that saluted the heavens.

"Pinche joto," my father declared each time Liberace stepped out into the stage on those rare television appearances we all looked forward to. Damn fag. My family was devoted to watching him because he was, after all, a great musician. An added bonus was that we could poke fun at Liberace's antics. I watched in admiration, envisioning myself swallowed in fur, thrusting my diamond-heavy fingers at the studio audience: *Thank you, daaaarlings!* Batting my eyelashes at the camera seemed so much safer than batting them at the bathroom mirror. Liberace could bat, pucker, wink, strut, and blow kisses with the wave of his hand. All that and Liberace was fat.

Aware that I had become an overweight child, I developed an intense insecurity about my size. My younger brother recognized it as a weakness of mine to be called fat names, so he called me a whale, sow, or pregnant hippo as a desperate tactic when losing a verbal fight. My father had started throwing in a fat name or two during scoldings but I quickly put a stop to that by threatening to run away if he kept doing so.

For me, the courage to step out into the world as an obese kid came by making believe I didn't notice I was fat, that my corpulent body somehow became invisible. Yet that fantasy was a delicate one, easily shattered when a cruel kid on the street yelled out "Hey, *fatso!*"

Reality had hit hard during a Christmas pageant in the fifth grade. Our homeroom was designated to complement a Santa Claus skit with the singing of "Rudolph the Red-Nosed Reindeer." As soon as our teacher walked in with a box of green and red elf outfits—a hat and a matching vest—I knew there'd be trouble. The hat wasn't a problem but when I was handed the vest I became dizzy with embarrassment.

"Why don't you just wear a green shirt instead," my teacher suggested.

When the day of the pageant arrived the following week I begged my mother to let me stay home from school.

"What's wrong with you? Are you sick? You're not sick!"

"I'm fat!" I responded.

I showed up to school with a green shirt. Throughout the entire pageant and especially through the singing of the Christmas carol, the stage lights heavy on my face, I knew everyone in the audience understood why I was the only elf without a vest of my own. The yearbook photographer even requested that I be moved to the back of the squatting chorus, or to the side at least.

After that incident being fat was the perfect scapegoat for all my other misfortunes. If I fell off my bike, I fell because I was fat; if I scored low on my spelling test, I scored low because I was fat. I was determined more than ever to slim down, to be as skinny as my large-ankled, knobby-kneed brother whose neck was so narrow it looked like his head floated above his shoulders. The ambition was there. The question was: how would I lose the extra weight?

For my grandparents, fat meant healthy; obesity was a status symbol. In México if you're fat, you have plenty to eat, and the money to buy it with. *Liberace—fat, famous, wealthy.* In the United States even the poor can be fat, because bad diets and junk food are cheap. When my brother and I first came to the United States we were diagnosed as anemic and were prescribed vitamins—big red pills my grandmother shoved down our throats with a jab of her index finger. Every morning before school: the pill, the finger, the gagging. We would laugh at each other getting subjected to this daily routine.

"I want you plump and beautiful," my grandmother would always say.

My mother and my uncle's wife, both big women, used to wrap their bellies with plastic to make themselves sweat when they did their stretches on the floor. Every morning I heard their swish-swishing all the way from the steps. But nothing seemed to change. They looked the same as their photographs in the brown stack of family albums. I imagined the disappointment on their faces as each picture became a testament to their failed attempts at weight loss. Eventually the swishing ceased, but my ingenious aunt found a way to compromise for the lack of exercise: a tomato diet. She'd skip breakfast and instead eat one juicy red tomato with a dash of salt. Later she substituted the tomato with a grapefruit sprinkled with a spoonful of sugar. When she tired of that she switched to chopped cauliflower with sour cream dressing. Then came the avocado with chives stage, followed quickly by the refried bean burrito with melted cheese week. And diet soda of course.

Instead of diets I was subjected to the infamous fat-burning cream my mother ordered for herself through an ad on television. Thick and yellow, it smelled like some kind of rusty metal—battery copper or a dirty butter knife. As soon as my mother applied it to my stomach it stung like acid. I jumped up and down, crying out, "I'm burning! I'm burning!" She pushed me into the shower then rubbed cold butter on my skin.

"Don't tell your father," she warned me as she treated my burns. "And don't take your shirt off." No problem.

I never took my shirt off in front of anyone because I was ashamed of my llantas, my stack of tires. I couldn't watch a Michelin tire commercial with my cousins around because they'd point out that I resembled the Michelin Man. The Pillsbury Doughboy and the cherubic Campbell's kids also sent me running out of the television room.

My mother's little yellow diet pills were another craze of mine for a while. But all they did was make my heartbeat race and make me crave food. They also made me lose sleep, and when I couldn't sleep I got hungry. I snuck into the dark kitchen late at night while everyone slept. I had memorized the location of the bread, the jelly, and the utensil drawer. I recognized the spoon through touch. If my mother heard me stirring she'd call out my name and demand that I put back whatever it was I had taken. I simply froze in my tracks, shut my eyes and pretended I was floating back to my bed. But the weight of the jelly sandwich anchored me firmly to the kitchen linoleum.

Soon my father got into the act. He suggested eating onions and garlic so that my mouth numbed its craving for sweets and sugars. My mother said no. My father had heard about this guy who had his teeth wired shut to lose weight and avoid getting kicked out of the Coast Guard. "Definitely not," said my mother.

"How about going out for a run around the block in the mornings?" my father suggested.

"And miss breakfast?" I asked in alarm.

My father became increasingly concerned about my weight. My mother's own obesity was contributing to her ailing health, and those extra pounds were dangerous to her weak heart. Besides, all that baby fat on my body made me look girlish. It was painful enough for him that by nature I was effeminate. I didn't dare tell my father about the kid who had asked me during school recess whether I was a boy or a girl. I actually answered his question, giddy with the excitement of being the object of his attention. I suspected my father hoped as much as I did that those diet pills would shrink me down to the gangly boy-shape my brother had.

"You look like you have girl tits," my brother pointed out. "Can I suck on them?"

"You fag," I said, then caught myself. How many times had I been accused of being a fag because I was this chubby, soft-spoken sissy too slow and passive in phys ed? *Move, you fag! We're going to lose the game because of you!* I'd come home, fat and frustrated, to bite into my own fleshy arms, admiring the tooth marks afterward with an air of revenge and accomplishment. I became resentful of the one boy in school who was fatter than I was. Alfonso never wore a belt, so his underwear and butt crack kept showing; he had a crow's nest for hair that attracted chalk; and once during class he sneezed so hard he splattered himself with mucous, earning the nickname Alfonso Mocoso. Yet it was me who was feminine fat. Fag fat. Even Alfonso recognized it. One time he threw his arm around me from behind and squeezed my nipple so tightly it bruised. Yet it was that violent grip that made me realize something about myself, because for nights I touched my wound, hoping to recreate that sensation of pain and pleasure—that gift given to me by another boy.

I kept my sexual desires secret all through middle school and up until high school. Meanwhile my obsession with my own over-weight body had intensified. I had mastered sucking in my stomach and pinching my fat until I lost my appetite. Obese people made me sick. Fat meant disease. Fat was fatal. I had known people hurt by their own large bodies. Like my mother. I always wondered if her death could have been avoided if she had slimmed down in time. Yet there they were, the fat people, taking up more space than the average person, complacent in their vulnerable big bodies.

I had shed plenty of my baby fat, but my weight fluctuated dramatically. I went through periods of overeating and even longer periods denying my body nourishment. I had no control. Other high school kids began to wonder. There were only two ways a teenager lost that much weight in my high school: through eating disorders or drugs. But only girls were anorexic so everyone assumed I was doing coke, crystal, or angel dust. My grandparents didn't know about the times I took my plate of food into my room and emptied it into plastic bags with sheets of newspaper, or the times I forced myself to vomit into the toilet while the shower was running.

My rapid weight gains and losses persisted throughout my adolescence. My grandmother had a number of explanations: it was latent puberty, it was that stomach virus going around, or it was depression. According to my grandmother I was still mourning the death of my mother.

My high school days worsened when I started struggling with my sexuality. I took refuge in books to avoid contact with the people around me. I read Greek mythology, first drawn to it by the erotic depictions of the Olympic gods on the covers. I absorbed E. M. Forster's *Maurice,* Herman Melville's *Billy Budd,* and Jack London's *The Sea Wolf*—all literature that taught me about disguised courtships and same-sex attractions, the pain and the pleasure of it. I sought out clandestine affairs of my own, which wasn't hard in a Mexican community, where it's possible to be a fag and not a fag. Men satisfy their urges secretly, confident that their public sexuality displaces any suspicion or speculation about their private one. Only men are allowed to use the degrading terms and callous words in the power play of machismo; women are expected to be polite, and not to even imagine the possibility that there is a homosexual locked inside a man they know. I had flings with married men or men with girlfriends, with men who had children, sometimes as old as I was.

They went to church on Sunday, drank beer, and eyed the teenage girls in gym shorts. They appreciated a good woman-on-woman porno. They showed me photographs of their fiancées and sent me wedding invitations. They were strong and loved to fuck big-breasted women. They were macho. I was their own personal Liberace who whispered tunes in their ears they could never admit to have heard. It didn't matter that I was fat or thin, just available. They desired me just the same.

"I wish you could stay with me forever," one of the men once said to me in bed, right before the phone rang. He picked up the receiver. "Cariño! How I miss you. How are the kids?" I never felt more invisible than on that mattress, under those heavy sheets that smelled of someone else's nights.

I snuck back home and made a ham sandwich, spreading the mayonnaise on the bread nice and thick. I savored it to punish myself. I ate it and made one more.

Everything I had learned to be and not to be, to accept and to deny, was finally derailed in the mid-1980s when Liberace began to attract suspicious attention. To me, Liberace had it all. His personality drew attention away from his obesity and sexuality. He was my hero, the master of disguise and deceit, the man who successfully showed *this* so that no one could see *that*. He was all things big: big name, big smile, big hair, and big shoes. One big secret. One big lie.

That lie slowly revealed itself as Liberace began to shrink out of public view—literally. He was losing all that weight, a feat he attributed to a watermelon diet. I remember my high school health teacher saying, "That's a terrible diet! Watermelon is ninety-nine percent water; Liberace's going to starve to death."

At first I thought I understood Liberace even more, that I was more like him than I imagined. I pictured him gnawing into the white part beneath the red meat or even into the hull of the watermelon, convincing himself that this was working—the pounds were coming off! I believed we had both fantasized about being one of those weight-loss product's spokespeople on television, the before and after images of their bodies liberated from the nasty cycles of weight gains and losses. He had created a new level of happiness I had always wanted: Liberace happiness—maybe fat, maybe thin, but always a sissy and always smiling. I wanted to own the secret to his success.

But then Liberace died on February 4, 1987, and that was just the beginning of his tragedy. The county coroner made the cause public: AIDS-RELATED DEATH.

The end of my hero was one big disappointment. He should have exited big, not amid the tabloid gossip and public paranoia. Matters worsened when a fat blond boy came forward as Liberace's lover and sued the Liberace estate. I was devastated for my poor outed hero. He should have shown me it was possible to be buried in the closet. I felt betrayed. Where would I go from here? Fat or thin, closeted or not, Liberace made it clear that no one could escape the demons. The demons knew hunger and bit the hand that refused to feed them.

Liberace sent me a postscript a few years after his death. During my first year of college I had lost seventy-five pounds. "They don't give you beans?" my grandmother exclaimed incredulously when I explained I was only fed hateful American foods like pot roast and vegetarian chili. There was much speculation in the college dormitory about my condition: it was rumored I had AIDS, and some students subsequently ostracized me. I became depressed. Thinned down, I had moved from one dark legacy to another.

On one occasion my father showed up with a two-basin kitchen sink in the truck bed. He acquired it doing a job on a former Liberace residence he was helping demolish. It was going to be thrown out anyway, he explained.

"Do you remember Liberace, you?" he asked me. I got goose bumps.

"Yes, so?" I responded.

"So it's his sink!" my father said.

"What do you want it for anyway?" I asked, almost stuttering.

"Are you kidding? This sink can get me maybe fifty bucks if I sell it across the border."

"Why? Because it's Liberace's?" I asked, looking for any distinguishing marks, for a candelabra or a music staff etched near the drain, maybe some telltale initial.

"No, it's nothing special." My father lightly tapped the side of the basin with a wrench. "It's just a sink. It's just a goddamn sturdy sink, that's all."

When the time came for me to apply to college, I kept everything a secret from my grandparents. I simply forged their signatures and sent the packet off, confident that I would get into that one college, the University of California at Riverside, ninety miles north of Indio. I hadn't bothered to apply to any other university because I didn't know where any of them were located in relation to the Coachella Valley. In my seventeen years I had only ventured south into México, and only once to the north, to Disneyland, on an ill-fated trip with my family seven years earlier. That time, the car kept breaking down and when we reached our destination, our stay was brief due to all the hours lost as my father tinkered with the engine on the side of the road.

When I received the notification of acceptance, I clasped the letter to my chest, feeling my heart implode. Finally, I had my ticket out. I decided to keep this news to myself, going as far as hiding the letter in the closet, beneath a pile of my grandmother's clothes—a symbolic gesture since my grandparents wouldn't be able to read the letter even if they were to find it. My plan even as early as the spring was to gather all of my clothes and take the Greyhound to Riverside. I knew the Greyhound had a station in Riverside because I had seen the name in the schedule display at the Indio bus terminal the times I took the bus down to the border; Riverside was a stop en route to Los Angeles.

In high school the approaching graduation was stirring up excitement among the seniors. I didn't care much for any of it since I couldn't afford any of the mementoes or activities offered for completing the four years. I had not attended the prom or the senior trip, had not purchased a class ring or letterman's jacket or the yearbook—had not even taken my senior portrait—and I wasn't about to attend the ceremony we had been rehearsing all week. But when the day came to buy the blue cap and gown, I got in line just like everybody else. All of a sudden I had this fantasy that my entire family would come to see me graduate. I was ranked among the top ten students in my class, which numbered well over six hundred, so they would be obligated to come.

Since the grape harvest was well under way, my father and brother had come from Mexicali to stay with us in "el campo." My grandfather profited by charging them room and board since he was not about to let them live in his home for free. He would continue to do this for many years to come, until they grew tired of his rules and conditions, after which they would find housing in an old couple's garage. But that year they still shared the room with me— my father, my brother and I, together again temporarily. I imagined them looking down from the stands at the high school stadium, waving when my name was announced.

The day before graduation I decided to tell my father. He had been puttering around beneath my grandfather's truck all afternoon, and was now rewarding himself with a cold beer. My grandfather must have thought my father deserved a reward as well, since he usually didn't allow beer drinking outside the apartment—one of the conditions that would later become a point of contention. The afternoon was humid; the heavy beads of sweat collected on my father's forehead.

"Did you know I'm graduating tomorrow?" I asked him directly.

"No, I didn't, you," my father said. "Good." He sounded annoyed, perhaps irritated by having spent too much time under a hot engine on a hot day. But I persisted.

"Well, there's a ceremony tomorrow," I said.

"You should have told me earlier," he said. "I'm busy with your grandfather's truck tomorrow."

"The truck is more important than your son?" I asked.

"For getting to work it is," he said.

My blood rose to my cheeks. "Why don't you go to hell then," I said before I went back inside. I immediately felt guilty, but I didn't turn around to apologize. Like every other time I had snapped at my father, I felt he deserved my abuse.

The next day, I dressed up in slacks and a long-sleeve shirt. I covered up the wrinkled shirt with a brown argyle vest, and thought it would be wise to slip on the blue graduation gown as soon as I arrived to the school, to cover up that drab-looking vest as well. I didn't even bother mentioning my graduation to my grandparents since I knew they never left "el campo" unless they had to. My father didn't object when he saw me take his car keys. I popped open the trunk to the blue Mustang, threw in the cap and gown with a hostile gesture meant to hurt my father, and then drove off on my own.

When I parked the car in the school parking lot, I opened the door, set one foot on the ground, and then thought how ridiculous this was, arriving to my graduation alone, without a single family member cheering from the stands, without a close friend sitting near me on the rows of 650 chairs arranged on the football field for the graduating class. I pulled my foot back into the car and drove down to my aunt's in the neighboring town.

"What are you doing all dressed up, you?" she asked when I walked in through the door. My cousins were sitting around in front of the television.

"I was going to some party, but I changed my mind," I said.

"Well, make yourself at home," she said. "We're going with Maggie to her son's graduation. You don't want to come along?"

"I'll wait for you here," I said, finding a pinch of humor in remembering Maggie's favorite phrase when she couldn't get her son to do his chores: "Are you a macho man? Or a macho minus?"

When they all walked out the house went silent. No one else was around. The evening was just as hot as that afternoon. I removed the vest, unbuttoned the shirt, and stood in front of the opened freezer for a few minutes. A gallon of vanilla ice cream glared at me from the back. I pulled it out and sat on the kitchen floor, deliberately dirtying my clean slacks. I began to shovel in spoonfuls of ice cream, and as it melted in my mouth, I let the cream run down the sides of my chin, like tears.

As the summer passed I counted down the days to my departure to Riverside. I began to fantasize about the new me: I would walk differently, talk differently, even sneeze and cough differently. I would lose all the excess weight I had put back on in the last few months. Without my grandmother to feed me, change was possible. I was going so crazy keeping this knowledge to myself that I revealed it to my brother, who wasn't really impressed, so then I told my favorite cousin, who didn't understand what all this college stuff was about anyway. She did, however, buy me a few vests at Goodwill because she had seen me wearing one before and she thought I should look grown-up if I was going to be attending an important school.

July. I turned eighteen: I could vote, buy cigarettes, and drink alcohol across the international border. But none of this thrilled me as much as what was waiting for me. I pulled out my acceptance notification and held it to my naked chest at night. We were becoming quite intimate, my ticket out and I. But then the guilt began to settle about leaving my grandmother, who had been, after all, something of a mother to me.

I decided to tell her the week before I was set to leave.

"And where is that, you?" she asked.

"Just up north, not too far from here," I said.

"Will you be coming back soon?" she asked.

"Of course," I lied. I didn't want to alarm her by telling her the truth—which was that I wasn't ever planning to return.

I asked my grandmother not to say anything to my grandfather, and she kept quiet. We had been sharing secrets all along, like the fact that she kept a loaded pistol safely hidden but easily within reach.

"What do you want that for?" I asked, frightened by the thought of my grandmother firing a weapon.

She pulled out the gun from the linen closet and waved it in the air, handling it like a sharpshooter.

"I'm not going to be like your grandfather, going to doctors here and to doctors there," she proudly replied. "The day I'm sick and useless I'm putting this to my head."

My secret was just as dangerous. I was leaving home, finally. I was starting my own life, finally. I was leaving all this behind—"el campo," my grandfather, my father. Suddenly the possibility of complete reinvention presented itself: could I even possibly change my name?

August. On the morning of my planned departure I stuffed most of my clothes into a large black bag that doubled its packing room by undoing a zipper around its middle. I had bought it at the Chinese flea market, where I also purchased a small box of detergent and a sturdy plastic laundry basket. My grandmother gave me an old faded comforter with lace coming loose at the edges and a beige iron and towel one of my cousins had pilfered from the Marriott Hotel where he worked. The last item I packed was an old portable Royal typewriter my father had found in a yard sale. He brought it to me the year before; it was one of his many peace offerings, and the only one that came in handy when I needed to type book reports or essays for high school. The black Royal came with its own black carrying case worn at the corners. I realized then that even these few items were too much for me to take by myself on the bus, so I reasoned that I could convince my father to drive me to the college dorms, where a room had been reserved for me.

My father and grandfather were sitting on the living room couch, watching television. I slowly crept over and made my big announcement.

"To where?" my father asked.

"College," I repeated. "In Riverside."

"Riverside?" my grandfather said. "I was born in Riverside, you."

"Did you ask your grandfather?" my father said.

"I told my grandmother."

My grandmother sat in the corner in silence.

"I don't understand," my grandfather said. "What are you going to this college for? Is it a trade school?"

"I don't know," I said honestly, but then I regretted saying it.

"You don't know!" my father said, agitated. "Then why the hell are you going?"

"Santiago's son went to a trade school," my grandfather chimed in, pointing his finger toward the back door for effect. "What a waste that was. Took out a loan from the bank and everything."

My knees started to shake. Things began to look blurry.

"No, no, no, forget it," said my father. "You're crazy if you think you can just pick up and go like that. You turn eighteen and you become your own boss all of a sudden?"

"But I was hoping you'd drive me there," I said.

"In the Mustang? It'll never make it all the way to Riverside. That's almost to Los Angeles."

"But I got in with a scholarship and everything," I said, knowing the uselessness of this information even before I said it.

"College. Can you believe this boy, you?" he asked my grandfather.

My grandfather shook his head.

I walked back to the room to pine away among my belongings. But I wasn't going to give up that quickly, not after waiting all these months. I quickly devised an alternative plan. As soon as my brother came in I told him what had just happened, and then I revealed the great escape: we would sneak out my things through the window, pack them into the Mustang, and then take my father's keys.

"I know how to get there," I lied. "But you'll have to drive back on your own. It's not that far."

"I don't know, dude," my brother said.

"Please, please, please," I begged, my body shaking, my sight dizzy with fear.

"Well, all right," he agreed.

The scheme didn't get past the sneaking-the-luggage-out part because the huge black bag couldn't fit through the window. My brother waited on the other side for me to force the bag through the small opening. We had already pried the screen off, but after pulling and tugging for a few seconds, a loud grating sound reverberated throughout the house. We had bent the glass guide out of place.

My father came rushing into the room, catching us in the act.

"What the hell is all this racket?" he said. As soon as he saw the comedy of our efforts, he understood.

"So you insist on this college business," he said. "Very well, then, let's go. But you're paying for the gas."

He took my bag and dragged it to the car. I followed with the laundry basket in one hand, the Royal in the other. My grandparents watched from the couch.

"Where is everybody going?" my grandfather said.

"To Riverside," my father answered.

"And when is he coming back?"

"In November," I said.

"November?" my grandfather exclaimed in alarm. "Such a long time. Then why does he need all those things, you?"

My brother rode quietly in the back seat next to the laundry basket since it didn't fit in the Mustang's small trunk with my over-stuffed bag. All the way to Riverside my father griped about how the car was breaking down, overheating, and getting its tires damaged because he was driving it such a long distance in the heat. The air conditioning didn't work, so our backs were damp from the vinyl seats. Matters worsened when we finally arrived in Riverside and couldn't locate the dormitories. We must have circled the campus three times before we came upon a picket sign stuck in a lawn, a black arrow pointing us in the right direction.

I was overwhelmed when we drove into the dorm parking lot, which was already overflowing with vehicles and people. All around me I saw families helping their college kids into the building, a parade of move-ins complete with "Best of Luck" balloons, teddy bears, computer monitors, matching luggage sets, and a slew of cameras and video recorders documenting the momentous occasion.

"I can't find any parking," my father said.

I was about to suggest he drive over to the parking lot across the street when he pulled over in front of the sliding door entrance and said, "Just get out here."

The trunk popped open. I got out and asked my brother to help me unload my belongings. My father didn't get out of the car or even bother to turn the engine off.

A residential counselor, an Asian man, ran over. "Would you like some help?" he said.

I looked over at my father, his face turned away from me. I looked over at my brother.

"I guess this is it, dude," my brother said sadly. He climbed into the front seat and closed the door. The counselor looked a bit puzzled.

"Later, dude," my brother said as my father shifted the car into gear and drove out of the parking lot, the Mustang getting smaller and smaller until it was tiny enough to fit inside a photograph.

The residential counselor took me to the third floor and dropped me off in my room. "Dinner's at six," he said. "Anybody joining you?"

I shook my head.

"That's all right," he said. "You'll soon find out how easy it is to make friends here."

"Thank you," I said. It dawned on me suddenly that he was the first Asian person I had ever spoken to.

He walked out of my room and I stared out into the hallway. My roommate hadn't arrived yet. Bodies shifted past the open door. When I began to unpack I thought about how lucky I was to have gotten out of Indio. I wasn't going to end up a farmworker after all. I had a good feeling about this decision even though my nerves were wrenching my stomach. The walls in the room were blank. The mattress on the twin bed looked new. And outside the tall trees were winking with the weight of fickle birds that hopped from one branch to another because there were plenty of directions to choose from.

Zacapu Days and Nights of the Dead

Summer's Passage

Once we board the third bus to Michoacán on our third evening, I resolve not to antagonize my father for the remainder of the trip, though all the bus interiors look exactly alike and it feels as if we're climbing into the same cabin containing all the negativity I've been dispelling into its air. We have approximately seven hours to go and most of that time the bus will be cutting through the winding mountainous roads of the region in nighttime, which I know will turn my stomach and keep me quiet. I smell the faint odor of roasted pumpkin seeds. My mother used to make my brother and me eat them with salt when we were little to fight intestinal parasites.

"Did I ever tell you about that time I sat next to an old woman who died on the bus?" my father says.

I have heard this story before, about four times. But I decide to let my father tell it by not answering his question.

"I can't remember her name anymore, but when you travel long distances like that, well, you know how it is. You make friends a lot faster. She talked to me about this and about that, and so did I. I wish I had had a tape recorder or something because now I regret not paying more attention to what she had to say.

"Anyway, she liked to talk about everything. She talked about her pets, her family, and her plants. She reminded me so much of both of your grandmothers. Not just because she was an old woman, but because she gave her words a certain flavor."

I know what he means: the taste of language that is only spoken and never written because the speaker most likely doesn't read or write. My father has it, too.

"She told me about how she sewed her money inside her quilt because she didn't trust banks. She told me about how her dead husband came to bug her on Sundays because his spirit thought it was still alive and kept reminding her it was time for church. She told me how her favorite afternoons were spent alone in a plaza with a piece of goat cheese on a slice of bread. I can certainly respect those simple pleasures."

My mind flashed through those imagined scenes of my father's poverty in childhood, of times my grandparents refused to talk about. The oldest sons were sent to scavenge the mercado trash bins for edible fruit, and my grandmother used to grow cilantro and chives to sell to the butchers. In those days, butchers provided all meat orders with garnish, and my grandmother was one of their suppliers in exchange for scraps.

"Well, if that bus trip had lasted two years, she wouldn't have run out of things to say. But luckily that trip was going to last only a few days. Even less for her."

My father pauses for dramatic effect.

"So the bus pulls up at a strip of restaurants on the side of the road, you know, like the ones we've been pulling into all this time. The people have to stretch and get some air. And they have to eat, why not?"

My father pauses again.

"And I ask la doña if she cares to step down to grab a bite. I mean, I couldn't guarantee her a piece of goat cheese but there were other good things: shrimp, enchiladas, maybe a sope with beans and nopales. Whatever. But she refused. She said she was feeling tired and wanted to stay on the bus to rest.

"I can't argue with her. She's old and she knows what's best for her body. So I go down and buy a piece of fried chicken, I think. No, I lie. It was a ham sandwich. Just like the ones that el Chavo del Ocho used to eat on television."

I want to roll my eyes at my father's embellishments, but I allow him to proceed uninterrupted.

"I speak to a few other people from the bus. We joke around a bit and exchange destinations until the bus driver calls us all back on board. Well, I walk in, take my seat, and notice the old woman is sleeping. I don't want to disturb her so I take a seat behind her, and I fall asleep as well. You know, nothing out of the ordinary. But then when I wake up the next morning, I realize that the old lady hasn't even shifted an inch. Which is odd on a bus, where you have to move every once in a while to keep your blood flowing. So I know something is wrong. I take my old seat again and I try to stir her awake, but she doesn't move. I alert the driver and he pulls over to check for himself. He confirms what I already know, that she has died peacefully in her sleep."

"What did the driver do?" I ask. I can't remember this part of the story.

"What could he do? We sat there waiting for the police to take her back to the terminal with her few belongings and hopefully find someone to claim her."

I squint my eyes. This isn't how the story ended before. In an earlier version there was a dying breath, a last-minute plea from the old lady to my father to tell her family that there was money hidden in the quilt. But my father was never able to play the hero because he decided to stick to his own journey instead of believing the ramblings of a moribund.

"And what happened to the quilt?" I ask, hoping to jog my father's memory about how this story was supposed to end.

"What quilt?" he asks.

I roll my eyes. "Never mind."

"Are you going to eat carnitas in Quiroga, you?" my father asks, quickly changing the subject.

I nod indifferently. I tell him I don't want to talk about food on this winding road. He smiles. I do love my father's smile. It's the smile of someone who could get away with plenty by simply flashing his perfectly straight teeth. My brother and I inherited our mother's crooked set. I imagine my father softening my mother's heart on a number of occasions as he negotiated forgiveness. I can't imagine my mother was as tough to crack as I am.

"Once we get to Zacapu we each go our separate ways," I remind him, deadpan.

"Sure, sure," he says. "That's what we agreed."

"And you can't come asking me for money, either," I say.

My father lets out a laugh. I think about all those debts my mother had to pay off behind his back. He borrowed five dollars here, five dollars there, and eventually the lenders—my aunts and uncles—came directly to my mother to collect.

"Look at that town over there," my father points out. "What would it have been like to have had a steady home?" It's not a question; it's a longing.

I look through the window at the huge valley lit up with different colors. The town is cradled by the dark mountains. From afar it looks as if nothing can get in or out, but judging by the stillness of the view it's as if the citizens have made peace with it and have settled without worry into their insular but protected haven each evening. There are people in the world, I imagine, who are born and die in the same town, maybe even in the same house, or bed. Creatures without migration: have they not lived a life because they have not moved? What of the migratory los González, moving from one place to another and marking every stopping place with angst? What kind of alternative is that? For once my father and I are thinking the same way, sharing a similar yearning for our starting points to have been different, for our final destination to be anything other than the tearful, resentful arrival it is likely to be.

And then a random thought enters my mind: I'm the farthest I've ever been from my lover. Each second takes me farther still. There are other kinds of distances besides time—there is space, there is activity. And so much ground has been covered on this journey, and so much thought has labored in my head, that my lover's image burned into my mind has begun to age, to fade. Is that why I keep bringing him back with the memory of our game?

"Ghost whisper."

"What did you say, querido?"

"Ghost whisper. When you talk to me in the dark it's like you're not a body anymore."

"Then what am I?"

"Memory. Purity. Honesty."

"And what does that make you, querido?"

"The rooms in your eyes. The rooms with the lights off."

"And what do the rooms with the lights off want to hear?"

"Don't touch me. Just talk to me. Ghost whisper."

"Ghost whisper *what,* querido?"

"You decide. But make it good."

Yes, querido, I will stuff myself inside you so that I can squeeze out everything you hate. That is why I have made up my mind to come back to you as soon as I return to Riverside. I can't leave what I love. Not for long, anyway.

What a fool. What a fool. What a fool.

I nod off to sleep.

At dawn I wake up anxious to get off the bus. The landscape has changed again into a constant spill of roadside houses covered with the haze of sleepiness that just begins to lift in the early morning hours. I recognize the textures of this waking up: a barking dog, crowing roosters, water gushing into plastic buckets, nixtamal, broom bristles, the lopsided wheel of the birria cart, old women's feet shuffling to church, their somber rebozos, freshly-baked bread, boiling milk, the crank-and-squeak of the first local bus, the compulsory "Buenos días, ¿cómo amaneció?"

My father's already awake and he squeezes my arm when he notices my eyes are open.

"I told you we'd be here by morning," he says. "Just in time for a warm plate of menudo at the mercado. You're buying."

I feel generous all of a sudden and agree.

When we pull off the main highway and into the streets of Zacapu, my heart begins to pound. The bell tower of the Santa Ana church (la Parroquia de Santa Ana) shoots up into view as the bus turns the corner. I stare at it until we reach the plaza with its small kiosk freshly painted for the Sunday afternoon performances. People walk the high sidewalks down to the mercado, the heart of the town, in steady strides. A pair of Purépechas with braids connected at the ends stroll side by side with rebozo sacks of corn. We have arrived.

Mercado Morelos is already full of busy shoppers and of merchants standing tall over their fruit and vegetable stands. Farther down are the canned goods and cheeses. Samples of the creams and raisins are passed out to the discriminating buyers. I have three relatives from my mother's side, besides my grandfather, who work here but I'm not expecting to run into any of them. The entrance to the restaurant area is bursting with the smells of freshly cooked beans, pozole, steak, and chipotle sauce. Across the way, a row of butchers chops the fat off the thick chunks of raw beef. The white spaces between the counter tiles are dark with blood, and in motion with flies.

"How about here?" my father says, pointing to an empty wooden bench. The cook hails us over. We haul our luggage forward.

My father orders menudo, I order a plate of huevos a la Mexicana—scrambled eggs mixed with the colors of the Mexican flag: green chile, white onion, red tomato.

"This is what I've been waiting for from the moment we climbed on the bus," my father says with an air of sentimentality when the cook places our food on the counter. "Now we can sit down like old friends and enjoy a good meal," he adds.

An uneasy feeling comes over me as I take my first bite of the eggs. My father rolls his corn tortilla the true Mexican way, by placing it flat on the palm of his hand and using the heel of his other palm to curl it tightly, top to bottom.

"I think of you as my friend more than as my son," my father continues. He blows into a spoonful of menudo before putting it into his mouth. He has this habit of talking one sentence at a time when he eats. In installments, my brother Alex calls them.

"Because when a boy becomes a man—"

"Apá," I interrupt. "What is it you want to tell me? You're starting to give me a headache."

"What? Me? Nothing, nothing. I'm just trying to make conversation that's all."

"We just spent three days and three nights on a bus together," I said. "Let's eat in peace."

"Fine, then," he says, looking hurt as he continues working on his menudo. But after a few more minutes he breaks his silence. "I did want to tell you one thing," he says.

"I knew it," I said, dropping my fork on the side of the plate. "What? Do you need money? Or do you want to charge me all of those damn cartons of juice you bought me? How much do I owe you?" I take out my wallet to add some flair to my theater.

"I don't like the way you talk to me," he says, his expression serious. "Full of anger and disrespect. How old are you now anyway? Eighteen?"

"I'm turning twenty in a few weeks," I say.

"Well, whatever, but you keep lashing out at me like you're still twelve years old. Isn't it time you let this anger go? I had my reasons for doing what I did, getting married and starting a new family. You and Alex were going to be old enough to leave home soon, and where would that leave me? With your grandfather all over again."

"Oh, so you left Alex and me to deal with him. You knew how he treated us all these years," I say.

"So you know exactly what I'm talking about," my father says, and his comment hits me on the side of the head.

"What are *you* talking about?" I ask. My face feels cold.

"About your grandfather. He's *my* father," he says, and then repeats it, softer this time, as if the phrase has become heavier on the lips. "He's *my* father."

"You mean, *your* burden," I want to say, but I don't. His logic is twisted, but abusive relationships do that to a person, turn reason inside out. It's the type of insufferable emotional bond that sends one fleeing from the house, from the country.

"I don't expect you to forgive me," my father says. " I'm not asking you for that. All I ask is that you don't forget that I'm your father and that I love you no matter what."

"Oh, sure, it's so easy to say that now that I don't even need you anymore," I say. "What the fuck's the difference after all that I've been through?"

In my mind I catalogue the times I wanted him to surprise me with a timely arrival during moments of crisis in which he never appeared. But my lip is trembling too much for me to give him my list in an orderly manner. I sputter out random instances, sounding incoherent and confused.

"Like that time I was sick. Like that time my mother was sick," I say. "And you abandoned us!"

I'm uncomfortable in the silence that surrounds us. People in the mercado make no effort to hide their curiosity as they turn their heads toward us. My father tries to lighten the mood by giving me one of his affectionate hair tussles.

"Leave me alone," I say. "I hate it that you can't even take anything seriously."

"But I know how you feel," he says.

"You don't know shit," I say. I blush as I add, "You don't even know who I am. Who I've become."

"I know more than you think," he says.

"Like what? What do you know about who I am?" I dare him.

"I know that—" but my father doesn't finish his reply. Nor do I want him to. We leave that knowledge unspoken because there are many other facts that need to be dealt with first, if ever. My lips are trembling and my father takes pity on me by looking down at his plate as he stirs the menudo a few times.

I finish my meal, listening to my father talk with the cook. It turns out she knows somebody he does, which is not rare in Zacapu. They kid around some and in the end she throws in a pair of sweet tamales for dessert, which I only pick at.

As we exit the mercado, the bright sun strains my eyes. I need more sleep and rest. I always surprise my grandparents with my arrival because I never tell them ahead of time that I'm coming into town. And after all these years there's always somebody at home to receive me with a warm welcome and a warm meal.

"Well, son," my father says. "Maybe I'll see you in the plaza some afternoon."

"I doubt it," I'm about to say, but hold back in time. "Maybe," I concede.

"I'm within walking distance," he says. "But I'll wait until your bus comes."

"What bus, you?" I say as I make my way to the taxi line, luggage in tow.

"Are you taking a taxi?" he says. "What for? The buses are already running. Look, there's one headed for Colonia Obrera."

"I'm done with buses," I say and wave him away.

"A taxi will cost you like ten pesos," my father calls out. "A bus not even one!"

I give the taxi driver directions to my grandparents' house. As we drive back to the plaza we pass my father, who blends in with the crowd except for his heavy black bag. My father says something but I can't quite make it out; I only see his mouth move as his hand goes up in a gesture of farewell. I watch him until he vanishes into the bodies of people going up and down the elevated sidewalks. These are the streets of my childhood. But they are also the streets of my father's youth. And of my mother's. He has many more memories burned into Zacapu's days and Zacapu's nights. He has much more to reckon with when he enters the town of remembrance. For me it is also about forgetting.

I challenge myself to remember the exact details of my father's tattoos: there is a three-leaf clover on his shoulder. The right one, I think. And it has a banner running across it with some illegible script. Maybe it's a date. He bears an anchor on his forearm. Small and sloppy, the flukes are not ornate at all, and the dark line going through the eye above the stock is supposed to be a rope, but it's more like a thread cut at both ends. And there's a third tattoo on his calf I can't recall. Is it a fat heart with an arrow lodged into it? I haven't seen it in years.

When the taxi ride starts to get bumpy I know we have reached Colonia Obrera with its cobblestone streets that slow traffic down. The taxi moves forward unhindered as it shimmies and rattles, jogging everything but my memory.

Ghost Whisper to My Lover

I think, querido, that none of us really knows how to grieve. It's such a mystery of an emotion that we trip over ourselves trying to get through this feeling of our bodies collapsing internally. But we have to fall apart in order to piece ourselves together again. Is it any wonder we love ceremonies, or flickering lights through our unknowing and the unknown.

When our former neighbor the hunchback died (his name was Tony, but my grandfather insisted on calling him "El Jorobado" so the rest of us called him that as well) the announcement was made at dinner one warm afternoon as the grape harvest was coming to a close. Tony and his wife lived a few doors down from us when we all lived on top of each other in Thermal, and their apartment was a favorite stop for us during Halloween because Tony was extremely generous with candy. He would step out on his front porch, dressed in a brown leather jacket with a row of fringes coming down from his shoulders to his wrists and across his hump. A matching hat with a tassel made him look elegant, even graceful. The news of his death came with a plea from his widow for contributions for the cost of the funeral.

The conversation then turned to the expense of El Jorobado's burial plot. Cemeteries were a waste of money and land, my grandfather reasoned, because after a few years, the graves became neglected, their locations forgotten, so that in the end the plot too became a ghost. He presented his evidence: his own parents' graves, his two daughters' graves, all *four lost in Zacapu's panteón. "Might as well toss the flowers to the wind," he said, "rather than waste your time looking for the headstones." My grandmother withdrew into daydream at the mention of the two daughters she lost in infancy. My grandfather kept on until he made his resolve.*

"If any one of us should die," he announced to those of us gathered around the dining table. "The rest of us aren't throwing money away on any burial. Cremation and a simple sign of the cross over the ashes is the cheapest answer."

"Yes, of course," my father added, always willing to add a touch of humor to a somber moment. "And if possible, we should get some permit that will let us drag the corpse out to the middle of the street to burn it. The only expense there is a sack and a gallon of gasoline."

In either case, my grandmother decided that we should remember El Jorobado for el Día de Muertos that November 2nd by lighting a red votive candle we bought from the Mexican foods section at Alpha Beta. The wax wasn't really red, but the glass was. The side of the glass had a sticker of la Virgen de Guadalupe with a bar code attached at the bottom, and it looked as if la Virgen were looking down curiously at the stripes.

For the first few years after we immigrated our family didn't celebrate el Día de Muertos because we didn't have any relatives buried in U.S. soil, and neither did we have a close relative recently deceased. Most of our dead were our ancestors in Michoacán, in the brightly colored cemeteries where we cleaned the graves on the first day of November, and where we shared a meal with the spirits the following day. The mood on these occasions was usually festive, just another excuse to throw a party, sucking on sugar skeletons and munching on pan de muerto—a plump bread with a button of a skull attached on the side, and a caricature of a skeleton body drawn on the top with sugar.

But November 1982 marked the first days of the dead after the death of my mother just two months before. One of my younger cousins pointed out that maybe we should do something to mark the occasion. I was surprised at how easily my uncle complied. He was the cynic in the family, known for his quick temper, his irreverent humor, and his foul language.

There were six of us gathered in the living room: my father, my brother and I, my uncle and his wife, and their eldest daughter, who had made the suggestion in the first place. We had no cemetery, no skeletons or bread, not even a marigold, the traditional Day of the Dead flower. In fact, the small garden outside my uncle's house only grew herbs—cilantro, rosemary, and thyme. The house was unpleasantly empty all of a sudden, the living room like a dumping ground for secondhand furniture: a television with an aluminum foil antenna, an old couch with sunken cushions, and a velvet landscape painting with a loose frame taped against the canvas to hold it in place.

My uncle knelt on the floor and called us toward the center of the living room. This was such an awkward gesture for him that even his daughter thought he must have been joking.

"What are you doing?" she asked, slightly embarrassed.

Surprisingly, my aunt and my father joined him, kneeling down to form a triangle of bodies. My father waved the rest of us over, and we did, forming an impromptu congregation.

"God," my uncle said. My cousin giggled nervously. My aunt threw her an admonishing look.

"God," my uncle began again. I could hear the effort in his voice. "Please receive in your glory those who have left us."

I was stunned. I never thought I'd ever hear that level of sincerity coming from the man whose favorite expression was: ¡Que chinge su madre Cristo!

"And please forgive our sins," my uncle added, finishing his two-line prayer.

He then attempted to make the sign of the cross, but he couldn't finish it because he didn't remember the verse that went along with each key point, so he broke down in a tearful apology that we all knew was not about the botched gesture, but about him kneeling there next to his recently-widowed brother. The rest of us, affected by the sight of my uncle weeping, also began to cry. There we were, six people on our knees, sobbing as one, as if grieving for the shared fate of our bodies sunken to the ground.

Zacapu, July 1990
(Imago)

As soon as I walk in the door, my grandparents smother me with hugs and kisses, an affection that makes me feel awkward. The banter that transpires between them is usually comic yet somehow intimate, as if no one else has a place in the conversation.

ABUELO: How is your father, you?
ME: Fine.
ABUELA: And your brother?
ME: Fine.
ABUELO: Isn't your president Bush as stupid as our Salinas de Gortari?
ME: Without a doubt.
ABUELA: You're still going to church, right?
ME: Of course.
ABUELA: Catholic, right? Not those fanatic ones that have you jumping around like you're holding in your bladder.
ABUELO: Both of these sons of bitches are taking us to war with the Iraqis. I'll bet my right foot on it.
ABUELA: Will you be quiet with your politics? This boy didn't come a long way to listen to all your nonsense.
ABUELO: (pointing at Abuela): Look who's talking nonsense. "Holding in your bladder."
ABUELA: This man is just waiting for me to die. So that he can get himself another old lady.
ABUELO: "Old lady." A younger one! And much taller too.

After the initial excitement over my arrival, my grandparents quickly slip back into their quiet routines: my grandfather pretends to read, finger on each word of the newspaper; my grandmother knits. They sit in the living room, lost in their intimate pastimes and speaking up only to ask each other for the box of unfiltered cigarettes. Here, I feel in the way, just as I do whenever I visit my grandparents in California. On the walls, I see the evidence of my past. Nowhere do I feel the traces of my present. I sit outside on the cement sidewalk my grandfather has elevated into a stone bench. There is enough space on the street for kids to spread out for a challenging game of soccer. There is a patch of unpaved road that makes an ideal surface for marbles. In front of other houses, other women sit to knit or chat before the mosquitoes start to bite.

When the soccer match is interrupted by a cargo truck that's getting maneuvered into a garage across the street, my heart pirouettes. After all these years I still have my crush on the neighbor's son. He has aged, just like me, but his hardworking life as a cargo shipper has toughened his features and his body. When he sees me he nods. I nod back. And then he drives the truck in reverse into the black cave of the garage. For the next week we will meet and make eye contact like this: me, his admirer, waiting for him to arrive; he, my voiceless adoration, coming home to claim my breath. Our history of clandestine glimpses is long, reaching back to the time of my mother's death, to the marching drills at Vasco de Quiroga. But neither of us has been brave enough to do more than yearn for each other from a cowardly distance.

At night my grandparents give up their bed to me. This is the most comfortable bed in the house, they say, and I deserve it after the long trek to Michoacán. I don't argue. This is the room where my ceremony begins. I wait until my grandparents say goodnight, and then I start to dig through my mother's things.

I don't remember when any of these photographs were taken, but I know what they mean. This collection of pictures was lost to me for many years after my mother's death, since my grandmother hid away my mother's two albums, afraid that my father would claim them as easily as he had taken Alex and me. The albums I remember clearly because I once made fun of their gaudy colors—swirling bright yellows and oranges with black shiny borders, like psychedelic monarchs. My mother had bought them at Goodwill, and they were now discarded remnants of a different era.

Among the pages is a series of snapshots taken during the California grape boycotts and strikes of the early 1970s, when César Chávez rose to national acclaim as a champion for the downtrodden farmworkers. In one picture I'm holding a red flag with the familiar UFW Union logo—a black eagle, or upside down Aztec pyramid, depending on how it is viewed. In another, Alex has joined the march, his hand held by my aunt, still childless at the time. Still another photo shows me with my paternal grandparents and their youngest son, all four of us standing at the shoulder of a road in front of the grape fields. Noticeably absent are my parents. But since my aunt is present, I always assumed my mother had been the eye behind the camera, capturing what can now be considered historical photographs.

When I first discover my mother's albums in my grandmother's closet, I have been looking for something else. I want to know the truths about my mother's sickness and why that surgery had not saved her life. I want to find out if there is something more to know about her sudden death. Perhaps the answer is written in one of the prescription records, hospital document printouts, or appointment reminders. All of the orange plastic medication bottles that had cluttered the top of the chest of drawers vanished the day of my mother's death. I have wanted to decipher their labels, hold the bottles tightly and shake them with my hand like rattles, twist them open, sniff the exposed powdery mouths, count the pills and tablets, perhaps even press one of them against my tongue like a solitary Eucharist. But they are gone.

I come across the photo albums with their records of pictures, many with people I don't recognize and many taken in places I have never been. These photographs capture an entire history that unfolded even before my brain began to store memory, and this history goes back to the days even before my birth.

Between the pages are also hidden treasures: old letters sent to my mother by her mother, each with a different handwriting; the newspaper clipping from my District Spelling Bee competition, my name underlined in red ink; and a series of plastic cards used for identification imprints, all of them issued by hospitals except for one. The red one with the UFW logo in the corner is my mother's union card registered in 1972.

With the farmworker strike pictures next to it, I suddenly have this image of a political woman raising her fist up in the air, demanding better working conditions and better pay. I see her marching in synch with the other farmworkers, their bodies linking together to create one palpable force plowing through the stunned avenue.

The only other time I recall my mother marching was during a pilgrimage the year before we left our house in Colonia Miguel Hidalgo to move to Thermal. The route went from la Parroquia de Santa Ana in Zacapu to la Catedral de Morelia, eighty kilometers to the west. Only women took part in these pilgrimages, offering a strenuous sacrifice as proof of their faith and devotion. At the end of the journey, they would kneel in front of the church to heal and pray, many seeking solutions to their ills or to the ills of someone dear to them. In my mother's case, she had gone to ask the Virgin to cure my father's drinking problem. Since the journey was long, most of the pilgrims were not expected to make it to the end, so a series of trucks crawled along with them to pick up those women who passed out from exhaustion. They were then driven the rest of the way and their bodies were deposited on the church steps. My mother was one of these women carried off, and my grandmother, who had been waiting at the finishing line of the pilgrimage, shook with rage for days after that, furious at what my father's drinking had forced my mother into.

I like to sleep in this room because this is where my mother spent her last night alive. She was not alone that night. One of her younger sisters had been keeping her company. They had joked that it was now the designated sick room because my aunt had been suffering from a leg injury and had to sleep sitting down on a small easy chair next to my mother in bed. As my aunt tells it, neither of them slept that night. Both of them were in pain and from this pain a sisterly conversation arose with the sole purpose of getting themselves through a sleepless, agonizing night.

"She kept repeating that if anything were to happen to her, we should look after her sons," my aunt insisted. "The last thing she wanted was for them to return to live with that hateful, greedy father-in-law of hers."

Throughout the night, the moon rained in through the window, showering the room with brightness. My aunt said that my mother would turn to the moon and her pale face would light up with white light. When my mother cried, my aunt had assumed it was because of the pain, but now she knew it was because of something more unbearable than that: the fact that she knew she was going to die and lose her children the next day.

I lie down on the bed that held my mother's body for the last time. When she was brought out of the car, already deceased, her body was laid to rest on this same bed and then was later cleaned and robed for the gray coffin. She had been dressed in navy blue slacks and a matching jacket, and a white blouse printed with colorful confetti bubbles. When I run across a picture of my mother looking out at the mechanical hippos on the safari boat ride during our trip to Disneyland, I recognize the blouse. Since she is turned away from the camera, the camera seems to be looking over my mother's shoulder as if guided by what my mother is watching.

When my aunt said that she and my mother had been talking all night without sleeping, I knew it wasn't true. That night I woke up to a murmur of chatter and I thought I'd surprise my mother and my aunt by crawling out of bed and joining them in the sick room despite the late hour.

I tiptoed down to the hall, the cement floor cool
There were no doors on any of the bedrooms, only th
which was why I needed to be silent, which was why I was positive I
had heard my mother and my aunt talking. When I finally reached
the last bedroom—the one with the window facing the street, my
grandparents' bedroom, the sick room—I discovered my aunt
slumped over in the chair, slightly snoring. My mother was sitting
on the end of the bed, her fists to the mattress, looking out the window and whispering to herself as if in prayer. I thought about sneaking up and tapping her on the shoulder, but was afraid I'd startle her,
and then startle my aunt awake as well. So I pressed my body back
against the threshold, hiding behind the thin curtain. I simply ob-
served my mother for a few seconds before I felt sleepy again and I
regretted I had wasted my time coming over. Now I would have to
steal back to my bed.

When my aunt mentioned the light coming in through the window that night, I didn't contradict her. Perhaps there had been light
at one point. But not when I stopped by. When I peeked into the
room on the last night of my mother's life, there was no moon at the
window and little light. My mother was a shadow of a body, more an
outline than a three-dimensional figure. She was one shade of dark
superimposed on other shades of dark, as transparent as a photo neg-
ative. She looked hypnotized, her stare fixed so steadily on the starry
sky that I wanted to sit down beside her and learn the secret of looking at the night through her eyes.

My mother gave birth to me when she was nineteen years old. This
year, on my twentieth birthday, I honor her pain by visiting her
grave. I buy a large bouquet of red gladiolus at the mercado down-
town and then walk all the way back to the panteón because mine is
indeed a pilgrimage. Anyone who sees me cradling flowers and heading toward Colonia Obrera knows this. My path is cushioned by respectful silence.

Summers are warm in Michoacán, but also rainy. In the two weeks since my arrival I have watched the sky darken each morning. Passing storms are furious with thunder and heavy with rain, but they don't last long. Like the many afternoons before, the clouds will disperse and leave the soil damp, the mountain air refreshed.

I enter the panteón. The grave keepers, four children and one supervising adult, quiet their chatter. They relax on the tombs. The trash barrels full of dry wreaths and other cemetery debris stand close by. I avoid looking at the structure housing the bier where the final blessing is given before the coffins go to burial. I pass to the left and walk back to the water faucet and cement basin. The blue tiles on my mother's grave have chipped in some places. Cans have been used as makeshift vases and have rusted, leaving behind a pair of unsightly rings. Because of the lack of plots, relatives are permitted to bury one loved on top of another. My mother's tomb was built over her grandmother's. I regard that photograph of my mother sitting on her grandmother's knee as prescient suddenly.

The simple white cross on top of her grave is as blank as bone and faces out across the cemetery to stare at the front wall. But the white stone book on the center of the tomb has her name engraved, as well as the dates of her birth and death. The book looks like an encyclopedia opened at the exact middle, and the two stone pages also mention the fact that she left behind a husband and sons. She lies buried here in the Panteón San Franciscano, but Zacapu is still alive with anecdotes and made-up stories about her. With each visit to my grandparents' house I hear a little more about my mother, and slowly I piece together this woman, trying to figure out if she would have approved of me as a gay man. In México the homosexual has many names: joto, puto, marica, maricón, margarita, and my favorite, *mariposa*, butterfly, an allusion to the feminine fluttering of eyelashes. To my mother, I was simply, mijo. My son.

Our time together lasted very little, and those last months were painful for all of us. The morning of our departure to Michoacán, my mother had been trying to change in her bedroom right after a shower. I walked in on her as she was putting on a bra. She faced the other way and I realized this was the first time I had seen her so naked. The folds of her skin and breasts were beautiful to me. She looked over her shoulder and slurred her words—a plea for me to help her with the bra.

I was stunned at first. The only other time I remember being thrown into a situation like this was when my female cousin sent me to buy a box of feminine napkins at the store on the corner. I didn't understand any of it: why did my cousin lock herself inside the bathroom and why did she yell at me when I brought her back tampons and not Maxi pads? What was the difference? Similarly, the workings of a bra were a complete mystery. All of those straps and hooks meant nothing to me. After much guessing and deciphering of her directions, however, I managed to maneuver the bra into place. My hands had trembled during the entire ordeal and afterward my mother thanked me with a kiss. It was an awkward kiss for two reasons: first, she had never kissed me on the eyes before; and second, a string of spittle fell from her partly paralyzed mouth and stuck to my eyelash. I was embarrassed to wipe it off in her presence so I simply walked away and rubbed it off after I had closed the door behind me.

I can only speculate on the reason she had given herself permission to trust me to see her naked. Had she recognized something about me? I want to believe she knew that eventually I would be twenty years old, a man, and gay. I want that gesture to be a sign of acceptance. I will never know because I came out to myself many years after she died. My mother never knew me as a gay man and I never knew her as the mother of a gay son. I can only search for clues and wonder.

One of those clues is the story about my teenage mother accompanying her father to charreadas, the Mexican rodeos. My grandfather was a skilled horseman in his youth and is still a good shot, he claims, with the hand pistol. Back then he enjoyed showing off his marksmanship as well as his beautiful daughter. My mother matched my grandfather's sombrero and holster by wearing her own charro gear, a denim skirt and riding boots. As is customary at such functions, one young woman is chosen to be the crown jewel of the evening. She presides over the horse parade and leans out of the judge's box to wave at the jinetes. On one of those trips to the rodeo, my mother was selected to hold that honor—to have her hair ribbons replaced with a festive charro hat stitched with sequins and silver thread. And on that night, all decked out and the center of attention, my mother learned what it was like to be a queen.

My recollection of that story is the only moment of levity in my daylong ceremony. Next, I wipe clean the blue tiles with water and my hands; I place the flowers as an offering to the base of the cross, taking a few to the graves surrounding my mother's because they had been keeping hers company all this time; and then I make my two-word statement: "Aquí estoy." I'm here. I don't talk to my mother or to my mother's spirit. She's no longer here. I no longer believe in God or in a heaven or in any fantasy afterlife. My mother is simply gone. The grave is no different from a photograph—a symbol of what has been, a memory of what has happened. I rest my palms flat on the tile. There is no transfer of energy, no sudden vibration or supernatural force connecting with my body. My senses are numb.

I walk back to my grandparents' house just down the street. Growing up in Zacapu, I remember visiting my grandparents and knowing all that time that they could see the white cemetery wall from their house. The road ends at the panteón.

I'm pleased to see that on the living room table my mother's sisters have on display the confetti Jell-O, a flan, and a pastel de tres leches. My grandmother has fixed a pot of mole poblano, my favorite Mexican dish. The smell of the thick chocolate and chipotle sauce thrills my senses. At my request, my birthday celebration will be intimate and quiet. As I make my way to the kitchen, I anticipate a cool glass of water to coat my dry tongue, but suddenly I see my father's image through the doorway.

"There he is," he announces. My grandmother comes up from behind him, a worried expression on her face.

"Give your father a hug, you," my grandmother says. "He came to congratulate you." She then says to my father, "He's so thin now."

I embrace my father uneasily. To my relief, he only sticks around to chat with my aunts and grandmother for another fifteen minutes before he announces his departure. And as he excuses himself, he asks to speak to me privately.

In the room he pulls out a small box from his jacket pocket and hands it to me. The box is illustrated with a black tuxedo and a red bow tie.

"I'm allergic to colognes; you know that," I say to him.

"But this is the good kind," he says.

I take the box and thank him anyway.

"Well, I'll be going now," he says.

"Okay," I say.

"I'm going to be heading back with my woman and the kids, probably by train," he says.

"I'll be fine," I say. "I know how to get back to Mexicali from here." The thought of returning by myself makes me a little uncomfortable, but I don't want to return with my stepmother, her three sons, and my father's young daughter.

"Well, I was going to ask you for a small favor," he says, sheepishly.

"You mean for money," I say.

"Not much," he says. "Just enough to cover the train tickets. We're going second class."

"You'll never change," I say.

I make a huge production of looking for my wallet and then of opening it. In a side pocket I have set aside what I was planning to give my grandparents before I left Zacapu. Impulsively, I snatch out all the bills and thrust them at my father.

"That's all I have," I say, aware that he has to accept this money on my terms.

"But what about for you?" he says.

"I'll figure it out," I say. "Take it."

My father stuffs the money into his jacket. "That cologne was expensive," he says.

"Of course it was," I say.

My father leaves, saying his awkward good-byes to my mother's family. He rushes out into the street as if I could change my mind at any moment and demand the money back. My blood is pulsing, and it's not going to be enough to cry or to complain to my grandparents. I want to do the only thing I know how to do—fly.

"I'm leaving tomorrow," I announce to my grandmother.

"What? Why? But you just got here, you," she says. "If you leave now it will seem as if this were all a dream." Dreamed words are empty words. My grandfather also objects, but he knows that they can't change my mind.

As a ceremonial farewell, I climb up to the roof of the house to watch the dark clouds creep over the mountains for the last time. Every roof is used to hang the wash out to dry. I sit with the sheets behind me as I stare at the life above the houses of Zacapu: pants and blankets waving on clotheslines, chicken coops, dogs that look down for the next passerby, clouds thick with rain. And across the street, the neighbor's son is piling brick. Each time he bends down to accommodate another pair, his head turns and we lock eyes. He removes his shirt in a vain display of his torso, which is smooth and fair-skinned—nothing like my lover's body in Riverside. It doesn't take much coaxing to find myself on the rooftop across the street. He spreads a blanket on plywood to protect us from the red grains of the bricks. The sky begins to drizzle. Not a single word passes between us when I remove my shirt, when I bring him down on top of me and slip my hands on his hard crotch, when he unbuttons my jeans and pulls them down, when we kiss, caress, and fuck with urgency because my hours in Michoacán are numbered. When the rain begins to pour I see that one of my aunts has run up to the roof at my grandparents' house. As she frantically pulls the clothes off the line she spots me lying across the way underneath the neighbor's son. I look back at her defiantly, but then my aunt turns away and keeps collecting clothes as if she hasn't seen two young men scrubbing heat out of their flesh. She's gone by the time the drops grow as heavy as old Mexican coins.

"I think we should go in, you," he says, placing his arm over his face for protection. He has broken the illusion. He has expressed weakness.

I roll over on my back, shut my eyes, and spread my arms out. The rain continues to pin me to the roof.

"I'm going in," I hear him say, but his voice seems distant, drowned out by the force of the rainfall.

It had also been raining during my mother's funeral. The mourners dragged in the mud off the street and every once in a while a woman volunteered to pick up the mop and clean a path across the living room. Funerals in México are also about drowning sorrow with liquor. The coffee is spiked with tequila and even the town drunks find a place among the mourners. My brother and I were too young to drink so we were fed constantly. We were sitting at the neighbor's table picking at bowls of beans when, from out of the shadows, an intoxicated old man emerged, speaking to us through his drunken drawl.

"Losing a mother is the worst thing that can happen to a child," he announced.

Immediately the other adults tried to pull him away, but he jerked his hand free.

"Then the father remarries," he said. "And the new wife doesn't treat you like a human being."

"Please, don Ramiro, please," a woman said as she tugged at his coat.

"I was only five," the old man persisted. "My stepmother beat me when my father wasn't around. She only looked after her own children."

He grabbed me by the arm, his eyes cloudy with tears. "If one day you should find yourself in that predicament," he said, "call on me. My name is Ramiro López."

At that point two men managed to pry him off me and lead him out of the house, but not before he yelled out again: "If one day! My name is Ramiro López!"

Later that evening I was watching my father sitting out on the street with a few other men. I could see him clearly through my grandmother's bedroom window, though he couldn't see me because his back was turned. I was trying to catch a glimpse of the neighbor's son who was unloading wood from his father's truck. He had been staring at me awkwardly for weeks. That's when I recognized Ramiro López stumbling around the truck and across the street. He came up and stood in front of my father, still drunk and slurring his speech.

"If your boys tell you she's beating them, you believe them," he said.

I wasn't sure if my father understood the context of his statement, but that didn't stop Ramiro López. My father looked around him and tried to conceal his discomfort with a weak attempt at a comprehending smile.

"You'll have me to deal with," the old man said. "My name is Ramiro López."

Again two men came over to escort him away, but not before the old man had the last word.

"You love your boys!" he said. "You love your boys forever!"

The pronouncement had been made on this street, calle Río Bravo, the street that ends at the gates of the dead like a modern-day Styx. Colonia Obrera had every river: Río Rodano, Río Colorado, Río Grande, and Río Copatizio. Perhaps it could also have a Lethe. I imagine Ramiro López's words disintegrating after all these years, the echo finally thinning down to fine dust breathed in, breathed out, and forgotten.

I think, *How clever time works, overlapping people's lives at certain stages, and as some eyes are waking up, others are already closing, securing the continuity of the world.* My mother and I were connected for twelve years. She also lived during a time I didn't exist. And I, in turn, must now keep living when she does not. And yet my father, who still shares the same wheel of time, is more like my parallel line.

The next day I will start all over again. I will board the bus to Mexico City and use my credit card to take a luxury first-class bus back to Mexicali. Two days after that I will hop on the Greyhound and disappear into Riverside. I won't speak to my father again for another year. When we finally talk it will be a brief exchange from that moment forward, nothing memorable, and nothing worth writing about.

But that's much later in the story. For now, I'm here, nude on the roof of a house in Zacapu. My hands under my neck, my knees pointing up at the clouds that are opening up in the miraculous way clouds disperse in Biblical illustrations. Light comes streaming down, comforting me with the realization that the sun has always been there, waiting, watching, and shining. My body is slick with wetness but will dry quickly enough.

Unpinned

Riverside, California

Each time I return to my ugly old Riverside, where I have never seen a river, only bumper-to-bumper traffic that shimmers its strings of headlights into the evenings along Highways 60, 91, and 215, I remember that this is the place of my learning. I would be more embarrassed to admit what I didn't know if I hadn't come from the kind of place I did. I didn't know, for example, that jeans came in different widths and lengths. I discovered this fact when, as a freshman, I tagged along with some friends to the local mall. I walked into a Miller's Outpost because on the back wall there was a stunning display of pants of all shades of blue and black. I zeroed in on the stickers on the cubicles identifying the design and size specifications. 32 x 30. 32 x 32. 34 x 34. 36 x 36. 34 x 30. 34 x 32. 36 x 34.

I voiced my wonder: "Jeans come in different sizes?"

"Excuse me?" the store worker asked, puzzled.

All this time my grandmother had been directing me to the Chinese flea market or to Goodwill, where the strategy was: as long as it fits around the waist, the length can be taken care of at home. I took these hemmed-up pants with me to college, and by the end of the year they were all high-water jeans because at eighteen I was still growing.

I didn't feel betrayed by this knowledge, or even ignorant, but I realized I had to keep these discoveries to myself or else I'd sound like a fool. So even though I was awestruck with the power of my first credit card (no one in my family had ever had one), I kept the giddiness to myself. I had no idea what most other college students discussed when they talked about music or movies or places on the cultural or geographical map. But I caught on quickly. Pretend knowledge was easy. And so was latching on to those people who possessed these privileged keys to the wonders of the greater world, like my lover, mi querido.

"Have you ever been to San Francisco?" he asked me.

"I've only been as far as L.A. Once," I answered, remembering my ill-fated trip to Disneyland with my family.

"Well, I guarantee you that by the end of the week you will have been to L.A. five times," he said. And he made it happen. Like magic.

I needed magic during my first year in college. The students I met had an innocence about them that bothered me. I felt resentful that I was carrying guilt over my shoulders about having left my family the way I did, about having forced my father into dropping me off at the dorms the way he did. I wanted to be punished. That too was another type of magic.

"I can tell you are lonely by the eyes that look like rooms with the lights off," he said to me. And I fluttered my eyelids, recognizing seduction when it happened, responding to it the only way I knew how, by submitting, by letting the older man, who has done all this before, do it again.

I need some of that magic now, I conclude as I move swiftly from the Greyhound station to the taxi to the housing complex on Blaine, which looks deserted because it's the middle of summer and most of the college kids have returned to the streets of their hometowns.

As soon as I enter my apartment, I drop my luggage on the floor and pick up the phone. The only trace of my roommate is the sink full of dirty dishes, which will remain unwashed until the end of the week. Of the two of us, he's the only one who cooks because I never even learned to fry an egg—not with my cantankerous grandfather in the kitchens of my childhood. My lover answers on the second ring.

"I'm back," I say to him.

"Are you hungry?" he asks.

"Very," I say. And we immediately slip back into our customary language of double-meanings and innuendoes. I become aroused simply thinking of his smell. I have learned to latch on to this detail because even after he turns off the light, even after the ghost whispers, I can still hold on to him through the musk on his skin. He's my quickest ticket away from the places I came from.

When I open the car door, the odor of pot assails me. I'm not much of a pot smoker because I get high on the first hit, which leaves my lover smoking alone and having to deal with my giddiness. I'm also not much of a drinker. After one cocktail I'm already relaxed and horny, which is perfect for an occasion like this. We don't engage in public displays of affection, but the compact car space is enough to make me feel intimate.

"How was your trip back?" he asks.

"Boring," I say. "The trip down was more eventful."

We rush through the meal at the local Mexican dive because we want to have sex. The waitress recognizes this urgency and winks at my lover when he asks for the bill as soon as she drops off a second round of margaritas. My lover reaches under the table and pulls my hand onto his groin. I give it the squeeze he asks for and feel the familiar fit of his semi-erection into the palm of my hand.

When I enter my lover's bedroom I seek evidence of other men and I find them: an empty condom packet on the floor near the bedpost, a cigarette butt on the ashtray—menthols, which my lover detests—and the scent of colognes that my lover would never wear. Despite this affront I find it easy to slip out of my clothes and crawl under his body. I remind myself that I wasn't loyal either. His fingers, rough as his kisses, press into my flesh with a fury that will leave traces behind. But I want him to remember my body this way. I want him to love me into escape. When he starts in on the butterflies I'm thrown into a fierce ecstasy that tells me I'm with another man's body, in another history that unfolds itself apart from my past.

"Did you miss me?" my lover asks me.

I take too long to answer. I want to explain to him that my delay is caused by surprise that he has asked this question first. I was just about to ask him the same thing. And doesn't that prove that we're on the same wavelength, somehow wired together because we belong together?

"Bitch," he says to me, and then turns away to his side of the bed, but not before he elbows me in the ribs. *El golpe avisa,* my grandmother used to say. You'll know when the blow comes that you have done something wrong.

I relax my body, defeated. I know this drill. He will wait for me to cool off my desire and then he will pounce on me at the most unexpected moment, so that the lovemaking hurts. I press my head to the pillow. Without my glasses I can't make out any object in the room. Everything is blurred and distorted, but I'd rather be here than anywhere else. And just as I'm about to drop into sleep, succumbing to my inebriation, my lover reaches over to clamp his teeth on my earlobe and pinch those parts of my flesh that hurt the most.

"I'm not going to let it go that easy," he says.

I'm not quite sure what "it" is. The fact that I dared to leave him again? The fact that I returned? Or the fact that I'm squirming and crying out in pain for a merciful release, especially when he penetrates me without lubrication? As his heavy breathing grates against my ear, somewhere in the back of my mind I hear myself think: *I deserve this.*

With classes still over a month away I spend too much time with my lover, enough time to know that not much has changed. Soon we are eating in the same restaurants, ordering the same dishes, drinking the same wines. Habit becomes us. I catch him staring at another man; he complains about my jealousy. I get bored watching him cut a rock of crystal down to fine powder; he gets exasperated at how easily I slip into a stupor after one small line. The only noticeable change is that he hasn't asked me to ghost whisper, the only part of our time together that feels truly intimate. This neglect makes me irritable. When I try to write about it, I can't get past the second line without tearing into the sheet of paper. Both my penmanship and my language are ugly displays of my frustration.

Since he must still go to work during the days, I'm stuck in my apartment, trying to avoid the heat in front of the air-conditioner. By evenings I have flung whatever book I was reading across the room and have crumpled up my feeble attempts at writing. I feel trapped and restless, and blame my lover for not leaving work early, for not coming to the rescue quick enough.

"I'll be there soon," he tells me. And I demand sooner.

"I'll be there soon," he says again, and I walk out into parking lot of my housing complex as if that will help. I get anxious waiting, and when he drives up, as I start to complain about how late he is and question his whereabouts, he rolls the window down all the way and he reaches out to slap me.

"You're going to break my fucking glasses!" I yell. When he strikes me on the face my glasses fly off. I have to wait for him to locate them because my vision is so bad I can't search for them myself. But he doesn't pick them up and simply mocks me.

"Get them for me, you asshole," I demand. I don't know if what is running down my chin is blood or mucous or tears.

"I want to see how long it takes you to find them," he says, amused. Through my blurry vision he looks like a mound of dirt. Out of anger I begin to stomp around, hoping that my foot will land on my glasses, shattering them so that I can't see anything anymore.

"What the fuck are you doing?" He opens the car door, bends down, and picks my glasses up.

"Psycho," he says when he hands me the glasses. And when I put them on it's only in time to see him drive out of the parking lot without me.

A few days later, he calls me and tells me to get ready. We're going to this party in Beverly Hills. "So look fierce," he tells me. I dig through my closet for a black silk shirt my lover gave me. I wear the black Italian leather shoes he picked out for me. Despite all this he never shows.

"All dressed up and nowhere to go?" my roommate asks me. He sits in front of the television with his feet up on the couch. I sit down next to him, kick off my shoes and reach for the bowl of stale pop-corn. This is roommate number four. By next month I will have roommate number five. All of my roommates bore me with their simple and uninteresting college lives. I move as often as I can be-cause I don't like them to know too much about me. As soon as one of them gets too friendly I know it's time for a change. None of them, as far as I know, suspects that I'm gay. I have outlasted the ru-mors from the dorms that I had AIDS. In college, where students come and go each semester, it is easy to outlive anything.

I don't hear from my lover for the next two days, and when he fi-nally calls with an invitation to a boat trip around Catalina Island I don't mar the occasion by reminding him that he left me hanging a few nights ago.

"You'll enjoy it," he says.

On the small boat, which belongs to a friend of my lover's boss, there are mostly gay men, all of them in their forties, like my lover. Most of them are with young men, like me. We eye each other suspi-ciously, as if we want to prove to the rest that we are more than a weekend trick. We don't speak to each other, but we beam when the older men address us. Each couple takes turns going down into the small sleeping quarters. When our time arrives, my lover makes a big show of our descent, guiding me down with his grip on my ass for the benefit of the other old guys. But once we're down there, he flings himself on the bed and leaves me standing there.

"I'm tired," he says. "I only have energy for you to give me a blowjob."

And I comply, because I know how important it is for my lover to ascend from the room a victor.

Once we're back out, it doesn't take long for my lover to get drunk and high. He claims a chair on the small, crowded deck and doesn't bother to look after me the way many of the other men are doting on their young lovers. Instead, he volunteers me to make the margaritas when the previous bartender passes out.

"He's Mexican; he knows how," he announces. And everyone laughs.

Begrudgingly I enter the compact service area and collect my supplies: ice, mix, and tequila. Outside the sky is darkening and when other party boats pass by there is an exchange of cheering and hooting. I'm excluded from all of this, stuck in the kitchen like the help. A few times a fellow guest walks in to grab a beer from the small fridge and feels obliged to pat me on the ass. And even though I run out of mix by nine in the evening, I keep making margaritas for another hour. The guests can't tell the difference.

The boat trip is the ammunition I need to antagonize my lover. I'm in his living room the next day, kicking the oversized vase in the corner.

"If you break that I'll break your face," he threatens. He holds his head between his hands, dehydrated and suffering from a headache.

"Go ahead," I dare him. "Break my fucking face. I'll kill you."

He lifts a finger up in warning. He thinks he can control me with one finger, holding it up to say what he doesn't need to put into words. But I've had enough of his stupid finger so I bend down and bite it.

Then everything goes black. When I awake, I know I need to assess the damage to determine whether I'm able to get up or not. The lining inside my mouth, behind my lips, has been split open where the teeth cut into my flesh. I run my tongue on the wounds and it stings. My nostrils feel clogged up and when I breathe I make a whistling sound. I have no idea what my lover has used to sodomize me, but I'm hoping it's still not inside my rectum because it feels as if it is. The couch has been smeared with blood. So has the side of the oversized vase. I have a faint recollection of doing this myself—marking any surface I could with the evidence of my lover's brutality. From the corner of my swollen eye I catch sight of the phone. He used this, too, as a weapon. Or maybe I did. I know that in the scuffle I managed to pick up a blunt object to hit my lover with. Perhaps the blood on the phone is his. If it is still working, I will not call the police or the ambulance. I will call Indio and let my lover pay for the long-distance call.

I reach over and dial my grandparents' number. The phone only rings and rings because, as usual, my grandfather has turned the ringer off so that he can sleep undisturbed. I lie on the carpet, losing count of the times the phone rings. But that's all I have to connect me with family. My father in Mexicali has no phone because the lines have not yet reached the outskirts of the town, which is where he has set up his home with his new family and my brother. He's completely unreachable.

And yet this is no terrifying realization. It's more like a relief to liberate my family and my father from all responsibility. What was I going to tell them anyway? This is all my own undoing. I alone am responsible for myself in my journey into adulthood.

How odd to be experiencing a catharsis lying on the carpet of my lover's apartment after he has beaten me to the ground. Nonetheless it has happened, this shift into something else. Once I am rested, I will rise from the floor and shower. I will walk out of this apartment and never come back. I swear it on my mother's grave.

Suddenly I hear a cough. My lover is in his room, most likely in his bed. I can hear him exhaling the cigarette smoke. The good thing is that I won't have to walk far to tell him it is finally over. I'm in no condition to move more than a few feet at a time.

I drag myself off the floor and rest on my side. I locate my glasses nearby and slip them onto my face. The frames are crooked, and the left lens is smeared with either spit or mucus. In any case I can still see through it, and I catch a glimpse of my lover hunched over the side of the bed with a white rag against his head. How small he looks framed inside the space of his door, which is ajar. He turns to look at me and steps forward to kick the door closed so that the slamming seals him shut completely. I can't help but chuckle at the gesture. But even laughing hurts my side, so I remain perfectly still for the next hour or so, waiting to gather the strength to walk away.

Ghost Whisper to My Lover

I'll end with this, querido, one of those strange tales in my life that I didn't have the chance to tell you during our nights when I wanted to share everything, when I wanted you to know and possess all that was me so that I could close the book of my childhood and call it a past. So that I could make you my future. But that was not going to be possible, was it?

Every one is a lesson. I present this story to you now as a token of for-giveness because there is never a forgetting. Because you too have a father you need to contend with for the rest of your days.

By the time I was a senior in high school I had quietly crept up to the college prep and honors classes where most of the students were white. All of the brown kids were crammed together in the basic and intermediate classes. And though none of the brown kids were my friends, I felt more alone and alienated with the white students. Among them I had lost my invisibility, my only defense outside of my home. The idea of speaking up terrified me. I felt somehow that I would say the wrong thing, proving to my classmates that my presence among them was a mistake. I'd hear them talking about their cars, trips to the Big Bear ski lodge, and their after school jobs. I had none of these things in common with them. How could I explain who I was at that point in my life without having to tell them the entire sordid story of the journey that took me there?

My ordeal only worsened when on two occasions, as I sat on the edge of a planter to read during study break, I was tapped on the shoulder by one of my classmates while a school janitor drove by in a compact utility truck.

"Is that your father?" I was asked.

I was startled by the question. The second time I was even indignant. The janitor, a plump man with short wavy hair and a pair of glasses as devastatingly ugly as mine, was not my father. We were both Mexican, but so were many other kids. Why was I being singled out with this question? Was I being ridiculed?

Since the janitor had been pointed out to me, I couldn't help but notice him each time he passed by. Perhaps I was trying to find some resemblance in order to convince myself that this wasn't some racist joke my classmates were playing on me but a genuine curiosity. The janitor must have noticed me staring at him intently because all of a sudden he started looking back. In fact, he began to acknowledge me by waving each time he drove by in his handy utility truck.

I became alarmed each time, afraid that the others would see this as a confirmation that the janitor was indeed my father. And then they'd wonder why I was ashamed of this fact, why I had denied it.

Now study break became a time of consternation for me as well. Since our mobility was limited to a patch of lawn, the smoking quad, and the planter, there was no place to hide, except behind the pages of my book. The print blurred when I heard the utility truck, and as it passed I prayed that the janitor wouldn't call out a greeting. I wanted him as invisible as I was making myself. Thankfully, he never made that choice and after a while I knew I had made myself clear because even when I dared to look at him passing by he didn't turn his head to look back.

At the beginning of the second semester another brown kid was moved up to the honors class. Part of me was pleased by this, but part of me felt a little resentful since I had worked so hard—an entire semester in fact—at becoming invisible. He was one of my kin; that much was clear by the clothing he wore, most likely from the second-hand stores. And now that he was here I could almost hear my classmates thinking: There are two of them now.

*I resolved to avoid him at all costs, which proved to be difficult be-
cause he immediately walked up to me during study break. And just as
quickly I resolved that we should become friends, compadres, allies in
this mostly-white classroom where students talked about weekends on the
beach and other mysterious pastimes.*

*He joined me at my spot, the planter farthest from the smoking quad
where all the cool and edgy seniors sat, only a few of them puffing on cigarettes. I was thrilled by the novelty of my company and glad to put away
my book in exchange for idle chat. That's what all the others had been
doing all along and now I felt strangely comforted by the act of belonging.*

*But this feeling was short-lived because when the utility truck passed
by, the janitor took up his old habit of waving at me, perhaps encouraged by the fact that I was beaming with happiness. My joy quickly
waned. And to add to the crisis, my new buddy actually waved back.*

*I had to address this immediately. I had to explain to my friend here
that things were different in the honors classes where we talked about
movies and called each other on the phone, where we discussed Chaucer
and Shakespeare, and where we used the same textbooks in geometry and
calculus that the intermediate classes used except that we were always a
few chapters ahead. Here in "Honorsland" we were united by our intel-
lect, not by our class upbringing, which meant that those of us who
climbed up from the bottom had to be discreet and quiet about our
humble beginnings. And we certainly, under any circumstance, did not
wave to the janitor. I would regale my friend with what I had learned. I
would inspire admiration at my knowledge in survival.*

*But as soon as I prepared to open my mouth, he looked me straight in
the eye and said with an uncontrollable smile: "That's my father."*

*Stunned and dizzy, I thought about my own poor father toiling away
at his backbreaking job in the grape fields or the asparagus fields or
wherever else he finds himself during the different harvesting seasons.
Where was my father at that moment? I had no idea. If anyone were to
ask me that now, I'd give the same answer: I have no idea. My father
moved so far from me I wouldn't know where to look. But likewise I
have moved so far from him that I can never find my way back.*

How wonderful it must feel to love a father so much that when he passes by it's like the sweetest reminder that you are not lost, and that if you should ever find yourself in trouble, all you have to do is wave him over.

WRITING IN LATINIDAD

Autobiographical Voices of U.S. Latinos/as

SERIES EDITORS

Susana Chávez-Silverman
Paul Allatson
Silvia D. Spitta
Rafael Campo

Killer Crónicas: Bilingual Memories
Susana Chávez-Silverman

Scenes from la Cuenca de Los Angeles y otros Natural Disasters
Susana Chávez-Silverman

Butterfly Boy: Memories of a Chicano Mariposa
Rigoberto González

Madre and I: A Memoir of Our Immigrant Lives
Guillermo Reyes